# Keto Chaffles

*More than 150 Delicious Low Carb Ketogenic Waffle Recipes
to Lose Weight and Boost Metabolism*

**Amanda Hayden**

# Contents

3

# SIMPLES CHAFFLES

## 1. Rich and Creamy Mini Chaffle

Servings: 2
Preparation Time: 5 minutes
Total Time: 10 minutes

**What You Need:**
Eggs: 2
Shredded mozzarella: 1 cup
Cream cheese: 2 tbsp
Almond flour: 2 tbsp
Baking powder: ¾ tbsp
Water: 2 tbsp (optional)

**How To Cook:**
Preheat your mini waffle iron if needed
Mix all the above-mentioned ingredients in a bowl
Grease your waffle iron lightly
Cook in your mini waffle iron for at least 4 minutes or till the desired crisp is achieved
Serve hot
Make as many chaffles as your mixture and waffle maker allow

## 2.Jalapeno Cheddar Chaffle

Servings: 2
Preparation Time: 4 minutes
Total Time: 10 minutes

**What You Need:**
Egg: 2
Cheddar cheese: 1½ cup
Deli Jalapeno: 16 slices

**How To Cook:**
Preheat a mini waffle maker if needed
In a mixing bowl, beat eggs and add half cheddar cheese to them
Mix them all well

Shred some of the remaining cheddar cheese to the lower plate of the waffle maker
Now pour the mixture to the shredded cheese
Add the cheese again on the top with around 4 slices ofjalapeno and close the lid
Cook for at least 4 minutes to get the desired crunch
Serve hot
Make as many chaffles as your mixture allows

## 3. Crispy Zucchini Chaffles

Servings: 2
Preparation Time: 10 minutes
Total Time: 15 minutes

**What You Need:**
Zucchini: 1 (small)
Egg: 1
Shredded mozzarella: half cup
Parmesan: 1 tbsp
Pepper: As per your taste
Basil: 1 tsp

**How To Cook:**
Preheat your waffle iron
Grate zucchini finely
Add all the ingredients to zucchini in a bowl and mix well
Grease your waffle iron lightly
Pour the mixture into a full-size waffle maker and spread evenly
Cook till it turns crispy
Make as many chaffles as your mixture and waffle maker allow
Serve crispy and hot

## 4. Simple and Crispy Chaffle

Servings: 2
Preparation Time: 5 minutes
Total Time: 10 minutes

**What You Need:**
Cheddar cheese: 1/3 cup
Egg: 1
Baking powder: 1/4 teaspoon
Flaxseed: 1 tsp (ground)
Parmesan cheese: 1/3 cup

**How To Cook:**
Mix cheddar cheese, egg, baking powder, and flaxseed in a bowl
In your mini waffle iron, shred half of the parmesan cheese
Grease your waffle iron lightly
Add the mixture from the step one to your mini waffle iron
Again shred the remaining cheddar cheese on the mixtures
Cook till the desired crisp is achieved
Make as many chaffles as your mixture and waffle maker allow

## 5. Bacon Cheddar Chaffle

Servings: 2
Preparation Time: 5 minutes
Total Time: 10 minutes

**What You Need:**
Bacon bite: As per your taste
Egg: 1
Cheddar cheese: 1½ cup

**How To Cook:**
Preheat your waffle iron if needed
Mix all the above-mentioned ingredients in a bowl
Grease your waffle iron lightly
Cook in the waffle iron for about 5 minutes or till the desired crisp is achieved
Serve hot
Make as many chaffles as your mixture and waffle maker allow

## 6. EggPlant Cheddar Chaffle

Servings: 2
Preparation Time: 10 minutes
Total Time: 30 minutes

**What You Need:**
Eggplant: 1 medium sized
Egg: 1
Cheddar cheese: 1½ cup

**How To Cook:**
Boil eggplant in water for 15 minutes

Remove from water and blend to make a mixture
Preheat your waffle iron if needed
Mix all the above-mentioned ingredients in a bowl of eggplants
Grease your waffle iron lightly
Cook in the waffle iron for about 5 minutes or till the desired crisp is achieved
Serve hot
Make as many chaffles as your mixture and waffle maker allow

## 7. Jalapeno Bacon Swiss Chaffle

Servings: 2
Preparation Time: 10 minutes
Total Time: 15 minutes

**What You Need:**
Shredded Swiss cheese: ½ cup
Bacon piece: 2 tbsp
Fresh jalapenos: 1 tbsp
Egg: 1

**How To Cook:**
Preheat your waffle iron if needed

Grease your waffle iron lightly
Cook the bacon pieces separately in the pan
Remove from heat and add shredded Swiss cheese and an egg
Dice fresh jalapenos and add them too
Mix them all well
Cook in your waffle iron till you get the desired crisp
Make as many chaffles as your mixture and waffle maker allow (5)

## 8. Crispy Bacon Chaffle

Servings: 2
Preparation Time: 5 minutes
Total Time: 10 minutes

**What You Need:**
Cheddar cheese: 1/3 cup
Egg: 1
Baking powder: 1/4 teaspoon
Flaxseed: 1 tsp (ground)
Parmesan cheese: 1/3 cup
Bacon piece: 2 tbsp

**How To Cook:**
Cook the bacon pieces separately in the pan
Mix cheddar cheese, egg, baking powder, and flaxseed to it
In your mini waffle iron, shred half of the parmesan cheese
Grease your waffle iron lightly
Add the mixture from the step one to your mini waffle iron
Again shred the remaining cheddar cheese on the mixtures
Cook till the desired crisp is achieved
Make as many chaffles as your mixture and waffle maker allow

## 9. Fried Pickle Chaffle

Servings: 2
Preparation Time: 5 minutes
Total Time: 10 minutes

**What You Need:**
Egg: 1
Mozzarella Cheese: ½ cup (shredded)
Pork panko: ½ cup
Pickle slices: 6-8 thin
Pickle juice: 1 tbsp

**How To Cook:**
Mix all the ingredients well together
Pour a thin layer on a preheated waffle iron
Remove any excess juice from pickles
Add pickle slices and pour again more mixture over the top
Cook the chaffle for around 5 minutes
Make as many chaffles as your mixture and waffle maker allow
Serve hot!

## 10. Crunchy Olive Chaffle

Servings: 2
Preparation Time: 5 minutes
Total Time: 10 minutes

**What You Need:**
Cheddar cheese: 1/3 cup
Egg: 1
Baking powder: 1/4 teaspoon
Flaxseed: 1 tsp (ground)
Parmesan cheese: 1/3 cup
Olive: 6-8 sliced

**How To Cook:**
Mix cheddar cheese, egg, baking powder, and flaxseed together
In your mini waffle iron, shred half of the parmesan cheese
Grease your waffle iron lightly
Add the mixture from the step one to your mini waffle iron
Add the sliced olives
Again shred the remaining cheddar cheese on the mixtures
Cook till the desired crisp is achieved
Make as many chaffles as your mixture and waffle maker allow

9

Servings: 2
Preparation Time: 10 minutes
Total Time: 20 minutes

**What You Need:**
**For Okonomiyaki Chaffle:**
Egg: 2
Mozzarella Cheese: ½ cup
Cabbage: ¼ cup (shredded)
Baking powder: ½ tsp
**For Toppings:**
Bonito Flakes: 4 tbsp
Kewpie Mayo: 2 tbsp
Dried Seaweed Powder: 2 tbsp
Beni Shoga: 2 tbsp
Green Onion: 1 stalk

**For Sauce:**
Ketchup: 4 tbsp (sugar-free)
Soy Sauce: 4 tsp
Worcestershire Sauce: 4 tsp
Swerve/Monkfruit: 2 tbsp

**How To Cook:**
Cut cabbage finely and chop green onions and keep them aside

In a mixing bowl, add all four ingredients of the sauce and keep aside

Preheat a mini waffle maker if needed and grease it

In a separate mixing bowl, beat eggs and add shredded mozzarella cheese to them along with cabbage and baking powder

Mix them all well and pour the mixture to the lower plate of the waffle maker

Close the lid

Cook for at least 4 minutes to get the desired crunch

Remove the chaffle from the heat and put in the serving plate

Make as many chaffles as your mixture and waffle maker allow

Top the chaffles with dried seaweed powder, Beni Shoga, Bonito Flakes, and chopped green onion

After that, spread okonomiyaki sauce and Kewpie Mayo

Serve hot and enjoy!

# SANDWICH CHAFFLES

## 12. Halloumi Cheese Chaffle

Servings: 2
Preparation Time: 5 minutes
Total Time: 10 minutes

**What You Need:**
Halloumi cheese: 3 oz.
Pasta sauce: 2 tbsp

**How To Cook:**
Make ½ inch thick slices of Halloumi cheese
Put the cheese in the unheated waffle maker and turn it on Cook the cheese for over 4-6 minutes till it turns golden brown
Remove from heat and allow it to cool for a minute
Spread the sauce on the chaffle and eat instantly

## 13. Bread Sandwich Chaffle

Servings: 2
Preparation Time: 10 minutes
Total Time: 15 minutes

**What You Need:**
Almond flour: 1 tbsp
Egg: 2
Mayo: 2 tbsp
Water: 2 tsp
Garlic powder: ½ tsp
Baking powder: 1/8 tsp

**How To Cook:**
Put all the ingredients together in a bowl and mix them well
Preheat your waffle iron if needed
Grease your waffle iron lightly
Add the mixture to the waffle iron and spread thoroughly and heat
Cook till the desired crisp is attained
Make as many chaffles as your mixture and waffle maker allow

## 14. Copy Chickfila Sandwich Chaffle

Servings: 2
Preparation Time: 20 minutes
Total Time: 1 hour 30 minutes

**What You Need:**
**For chicken:**

Chicken Breast: 1
Parmesan cheese: 4 tbsp
Dill pickle juice: 4 tbsp
Pork rinds: 2 tbsp
Flax seed: 1 tsp (grounded)
Butter: 1 tsp

Salt: ¼ tsp or as per your taste

Black pepper: ¼ tsp or as per your taste

**For Sandwich Bun:**

Egg: 1

Mozzarella Cheese: 1 cup (shredded)

Stevia glycerite: 4 drops

Butter extract: ¼ tsp

**How To Cook:**

Cut chicken into half-inch pieces and add in a ziplock bag with pickle juice

Keep them together for an hour to overnight

Preheat the air fryer for five minutes

In a mixing bowl add all the chicken ingredients and mix well

Now add the chicken and discard the pickle juice

Cook the chicken in the air fryer at 400 degrees for 6 minutes from each side and set aside

Mix all the sandwich bun ingredients in a bowl

Put the mixture to the mini waffle maker and cook for 4 minutes

Remove from heat

Make the chaffle sandwich by adding the prepared chicken in between

## 15. Chaffle Sandwich with Eggs and Bacon

Servings: 2

Preparation Time: 5 minutes

Total Time: 10 minutes

**What You Need:**

**For Chaffles:**

Egg: 2

Cheddar cheese: 1 cup (shredded)

**For Sandwich:**

Bacon strips: 4

American cheese: 2 slices

Egg: 2

**How To Cook:**

Preheat a mini waffle maker if needed and grease it

In a mixing bowl, beat eggs and add shredded cheddar cheese to them

Mix them all well and pour the mixture to the lower plate of the waffle maker

Close the lid

Cook for at least 4 minutes to get the desired crunch

In the meanwhile, cook slices on bacon on medium flame in a large non-stick pan till they turn crispy and pat dry with a paper towel after removing them

In the same pan, fry eggs

Remove the chaffle from the heat

Make as many chaffles as your mixture and waffle maker allow

Assemble slices of bacon, egg and cheese slice in between the two chaffles and enjoy!

## 16. Keto Sandwich Chaffle

Servings: 2
Preparation Time: 5 minutes
Total Time: 10 minutes

**What You Need:**
Egg: 2
Cheddar cheese: 1 cup shredded
Almond flour: 2 tbsp

**How To Cook:**
Preheat a mini waffle iron if needed
In a mixing bowl, beat eggs and add cheddar cheese to them
To enhance the texture, add almond flour to it
Mix them all well and pour to the greasy mini waffle iron
Cook for at least 4 minutes to get the desired crunch
Remove the chaffle from the heat and keep aside for around one minute
Take two chaffles and place your favorite garnishing in between to make a sandwich
Make as many chaffles as your mixture and waffle maker allow

## 17. BLT Chaffle

Servings: 2
Preparation Time: 5 minutes
Total Time: 10 minutes
**What You Need:**
**For Chaffles:**
Egg: 2
Mozzarella cheese: 1 cup (shredded)
Green onion: 1 tbsp (diced)
Italian seasoning: ½ tsp

**For Sandwich:**
Bacon strips: 4
Lettuce leaves: 2
Tomato: 1 sliced
Mayo: 2 tbs

**How To Cook:**
Preheat a mini waffle maker if needed and grease it
In a mixing bowl, beat eggs and add all the ingredients to it
Mix them all well
Pour the mixture to the lower plate of the waffle maker and spread it evenly to cover the plate properly
Close the lid
Cook for at least 4 minutes to get the desired crunch
Remove the chaffle from the heat and keep aside for around one minute
Make as many chaffles as your mixture and waffle maker allow
Serve with bacon, lettuce, mayo, and tomato in between two chaffles

Servings: 2
Preparation Time: 20 minutes
Total Time: 1 hour 30 minutes

## What You Need:
### For Chaffle:
Egg: 2
Mozzarella cheese: 1 cup (shredded)
Green leaf lettuce: 2 leaves (optional)

### For Sauce:
Ketchup: 2 tbsp (sugar-free)
Oyster Sauce: 1 tbsp
Worcestershire Sauce: 2 tbsp
Swerve/Monkfruit: 1 tsp

### For Chicken:
Chicken thigh: 2 pieces boneless or ¼ lb boneless
Almond flour: 1 cup
Egg: 1
Salt: ¼ tsp or as per your taste
Black pepper: ¼ tsp or as per your taste
Pork Rinds: 3 oz. unflavored
Vegetable oil: 2 cups for deep frying

### Brine:
Water: 2 cups
Salt: 1 tbsp

## How To Cook:
In a pot, cook the chicken by adding two cups of water to it with salt and bring to boil

Close the lid of the pot and cook for 30 minutes

Pat dry the chicken by using a kitchen towel and add salt and black pepper to both sides

In a mixing bowl, add sugar-free ketchup, oyster sauce, Swerve/Monkfruit, and Worcestershire sauce; combine them well and set aside to put it in the sandwich later

Grind unflavored pork rinds in a food processor and turn into very fine crumbs

Take three mixing bowls and add almond flour in 1 bowl, beaten eggs in 1 bowl, and crushed pork rinds to the last one

Coat the chicken pieces in this order: almond flour then eggs then crushed pork rinds and set aside

In a deep frying pan, pour enough oil that can dip chicken pieces and heat it

When done, add coated chicken pieces and fry till they turn golden brown

Transfer chicken to the drying rack to remove excess oil

Preheat a mini waffle maker if needed

In a mixing bowl, beat eggs and add mozzarella cheese to them

Mix them all well and pour to the greasy mini waffle maker

Cook for at least 4 minutes to get the desired crunch

Remove the chaffle from the heat and keep aside for around one minute

Make as many chaffles as your mixture and waffle maker allow

Wash green leaf lettuces and dry them Now take one chaffle, spread the sauce on it (that was prepared previously), place green lettuce on it, then a chicken katsu, and lastly another chaffle piece

Serve hot and enjoy!

## 19. Three Vegetable Sandwich Chaffle

Servings: 2
Preparation Time: 10 minutes
Total Time: 20 minutes

**What You Need:**
**For Chaffle:**
Egg: 2
Mozzarella cheese: 1 cup (shredded)

**For Vegetables:**
Onion: 1 small (Sliced)
Tomato: 1 small (sliced)
Cauliflower: 1 cup
Salt: ¼ tsp or as per your taste
Black pepper: ¼ tsp or as per your taste

**For Sauce:**
Ketchup: 2 tbsp (sugar-free)
Oyster Sauce: 1 tbsp
Worcestershire Sauce: 2 tbsp
Swerve/Monkfruit: 1 tsp

**How To Cook:**
In a mixing bowl, add sugar-free ketchup, oyster sauce, Swerve/Monkfruit, and Worcestershire sauce; combine them well and set aside to put it in the sandwich later

Boil cauliflower in ample amount of water and strain

Add salt and pepper to taste and blend and set aside

Preheat a mini waffle maker if needed and grease it

In a mixing bowl, beat eggs and add all the chaffle ingredients

Mix them all well

Pour the mixture to the lower plate of the waffle maker and spread it evenly to cover the plate properly

Close the lid

Cook for at least 4 minutes to get the desired crunch

Remove the chaffle from the heat and keep aside for around one minute

Make as many chaffles as your mixture and waffle maker allow

Serve with the sauce you prepared and the three vegetables in between two chaffles

Serve hot and enjoy!

## 20. Keto Pepperoni Chaffle Pizza

Servings: 2
Preparation Time: 10 minutes
Total Time: 15 minutes

**What You Need:**

**For Pizza Chaffles:**

Eggs: 2
Cheddar cheese: ½ cup
Parmesan cheese: 2 tbsp
Italian season: ¼ tsp

**For Toppings:**

Tomato sauce: 2 tsp (sugar-free)
Mozzarella cheese: ½ cup shredded
Pepperoni slices: 8

**How To Cook:**

Preheat your waffle iron

In mixing bowl, add all the pizza chaffles ingredients and mix well

Grease your waffle iron lightly

Pour the mixture to the bottom plate evenly; also spread it out to get better results

Close the upper plate and heat

Cook for 6 minutes or until the chaffle is done

Make as many chaffles as your mixture and waffle maker allow

Lift the lid and place the chaffle on the baking tray lined with parchment paper

On each chaffle, spread tomato sauce and place pepperoni slices

Sprinkle mozzarella cheese at the end

Bake for two minutes till the cheese turns brown

## 21. Japanese Style Chaffle Pizza

Servings: 2
Preparation Time: 5 minutes
Total Time: 10 minutes

**What You Need:**

**For Crust:**

Egg: 2
Mozzarella cheese: 1 cup (shredded)

**For Toppings:**

Pizza sauce: 4 tbsp
Mozzarella cheese: 2 tbsp (shredded)
Japanese sausage: 2 whole
Kewpie mayo: 2 tbsp
Asparagus: 2 stalks
Dried seaweed: 2 tsp

**How To Cook:**

Preheat a mini waffle maker if needed and grease it

In a mixing bowl, beat eggs and add mozzarella cheese to them

Mix them all well and pour the mixture to the lower plate of the waffle maker

Close the lid

Cook for at least 4 minutes to get the desired crunch

In the meantime, prepare pizza toppings by slicing asparagus to ¼ inch slice and Japanese sausages

Preheat oven to 500F

Remove the chaffle from the heat and place them on the baking tray

One each chaffle, spread pizza sauce and add a bit of mozzarella cheese followed by asparagus, Japanese sausage, and Kewpie mayo

Place the tray into the oven and bake for 3-5 minutes at the same temperature till the cheese melts

Serve with shredded dried seaweed on top and enjoy

Make as many chaffles as your mixture and waffle maker allow

## 22. Desi Style Chicken Pizza Chaffles

Servings: 2

Preparation Time: 15 minutes

Total Time: 25 minutes

**What You Need:**

**For Pizza Chaffles:**

Eggs: 2

Cheddar cheese: ½ cup

Parmesan cheese: 2 tbsp

Italian season: ¼ tsp

**For Toppings:**

Tomato sauce: 2 tsp (sugar-free)

Mozzarella cheese: ½ cup shredded

**For Desi Chicken:**

Small chicken boneless cubes: 1 cup

Garlic: 1 tbsp minced

Onion powder: 1 tbsp

Salt: ¼ tsp or as per your taste

Black pepper: ¼ tsp or as per your taste

Red chili flakes: ¼ tsp

Butter: 2 tbsp

**How To Cook:**

Preheat your waffle iron

In mixing bowl, add all the pizza chaffle ingredients and mix well

Grease your waffle iron lightly

Pour the mixture to the bottom plate evenly; also spread it out to get better results

Close the upper plate and heat

Cook for 6 minutes or until the chaffle is done

Make as many chaffles as your mixture and waffle maker allow

In the meanwhile, in a small saucepan melt butter and add garlic minced and stir for 30 seconds

Add chicken cubes with all other seasoning and mix well

Cook for around 10 minutes on medium-low heat

Remove from heat and set aside

Lift the lid and place the chaffle on the baking tray lined with parchment paper

On each chaffle, spread tomato sauce and place 5-6 chicken cubes

Sprinkle mozzarella cheese at the end

Bake for two minutes till the cheese turns brown

## 23. BBQ Chicken Pizza Chaffle

Servings: 2
Preparation Time: 15 minutes
Total Time: 25 minutes

**What You Need:**
**For Pizza Chaffles:**
Eggs: 2
Cheddar cheese: ½ cup
Parmesan cheese: 2 tbsp
Italian season: ¼ tsp
**For Toppings:**
Tomato sauce: 2 tsp (sugar-free)
Mozzarella cheese: ½ cup shredded
**For BBQ Chicken:**
Chicken: 1/2 cup
BBQ sauce: 1 tbsp (sugar-free)
Butter: 1 tbsp

**How To Cook:**
Preheat your waffle iron
In mixing bowl, add all the pizza chaffle ingredients and mix well
Grease your waffle iron lightly
Pour the mixture to the bottom plate evenly; also spread it out to get better results and close the upper plate and heat
Cook for 6 minutes or until the chaffle is done
Make as many chaffles as your mixture and waffle maker allow
In the meanwhile, melt butter in a pan and add diced chicken
Cook for around 10 minutes on medium-low heat
Remove from heat, add bbq sauce and set aside
Lift the lid and place the chaffle on the baking tray lined with parchment paper
On each chaffle, spread tomato sauce and place 5-6 chicken cubes
Sprinkle mozzarella cheese at the end
Bake for two minutes till the cheese turns brown

## 24. Keto Cauliflower Onion Pizza Chaffle

Servings: 2
Preparation Time: 10 minutes
Total Time: 15 minutes

**What You Need:**
**For Pizza Chaffles:**
Eggs: 2
Cheddar cheese: ½ cup
Parmesan cheese: 2 tbsp
Italian season: ¼ tsp

**For Toppings:**

Tomato sauce: 2 tsp (sugar-free)
Mozzarella cheese: ½ cup shredded
Cauliflower: 1 cup (cut in cubes)
Onion: ½ cup (cut in cubes)
Butter: 1 tbsp
Salt: a pinch

**How To Cook:**

In a small saucepan, melt one tablespoon of butter and add cauliflower to it

Stir for 5 minutes and add onion and stir for two minutes more and set aside

Preheat your waffle iron

In mixing bowl, add all the pizza chaffle ingredients and mix well

Grease your waffle iron lightly

Pour the mixture to the bottom plate evenly; also spread it out to get better results

Close the upper plate and heat

Cook for 6 minutes or until the chaffle is done

Make as many chaffles as your mixture and waffle maker allow

Lift the lid and place the chaffle on the baking tray lined with parchment paper

On each chaffle, spread tomato sauce and place diced cauliflower and onion

Sprinkle mozzarella cheese at the end

Bake for two minutes till the cheese turns brown

## 25. Simple Vegetable Pizza Chaffle

Servings: 2

Preparation Time: 15 minutes

Total Time: 25 minutes

**What You Need:**

**For Pizza Chaffles:**

Eggs: 2

Cheddar cheese: ½ cup

Parmesan cheese: 2 tbsp

Italian season: ¼ tsp

**For Toppings:**

Tomato sauce: 2 tsp (sugar-free)

Mozzarella cheese: ½ cup shredded

Cauliflower: 4 tbsp (cut in cubes)

Onion: 4 tbsp (cut in cubes)

Olives: 4 tbsp (cut in cubes)

Red pepper: 4 tbsp (cut in cubes)

Tomatoes: 4 tbsp (cut in cubes)

Butter: 1 tbsp

Salt: a pinch

**How To Cook:**

Take a small saucepan and add butter

Add onion, red pepper, tomatoes, and cauliflower

Sauté the vegetables for 4 minutes, add salt, and set aside

In a separate pan, mix all the chaffle ingredients

Cook in the waffle maker for over 4 minutes

Now remove from heat and put on the baking tray

Spread tomato sauce on the chaffle

Place the vegetables on the chaffles and sprinkle cheese

Bake for 5 minutes or till the cheese melt

Serve hot

## 26. Sausage Biscuits and Gravy Breakfast Chaffle

Serving: 2
Preparation Time: 10 minutes
Total Time: 20 minutes

**What You Need:**
Egg: 2
Mozzarella cheese: 1 cup
Onion: ¼ tbsp (granulated)
Garlic: ¼ tbsp (granulated)
Butter: 2 tbsp
Garlic: 1 tbsp (finely minced)
Almond flour: 1 tbsp
Cornbread starch: 10 drops
Baking powder: 1 tsp
Dried parsley: 1 tsp
Keto sausage biscuit and gravy: 1 batch

**How To Cook:**
Preheat a mini waffle maker if needed and grease it
In a mixing bowl, beat eggs and add all the chaffle ingredients except the last one
Mix them all well
Pour the mixture to the lower plate of the waffle maker and spread it evenly to cover the plate properly
Close the lid
Cook for at least 4 minutes to get the desired crunch
Remove the chaffle from the heat and keep aside
Make as many chaffles as your mixture and waffle maker allow
Prepare Sausage Gravy recipe and serve with yummy chaffles

## 27. Mushroom Stuffed Chaffles

Servings: 2
Preparation Time: 15 minutes
Total Time: 40 minutes

**What You Need:**
**For Chaffle:**
Egg: 2
Mozzarella Cheese: ½ cup (shredded)
Onion powder: ½ tsp
Garlic powder: ¼ tsp
Salt: ¼ tsp or as per your taste

Black pepper: ¼ tsp or as per your taste
Dried poultry seasoning: ½ tsp
**For Stuffing:**
Onion: 1 small diced
Mushrooms: 4 oz.
Celery stalks: 3
Butter: 4 tbsp
Eggs: 3

**How To Cook:**

Preheat a mini waffle maker if needed and grease it

In a mixing bowl, add all the chaffle ingredients

Mix them all well

Pour the mixture to the lower plate of the waffle maker and spread it evenly to cover the plate properly and close the lid

Cook for at least 4 minutes to get the desired crunch

Remove the chaffle from the heat and keep aside

Make as many chaffles as your mixture and waffle maker allow

Take a small frying pan and melt butter in it on medium-low heat

Sauté celery, onion, and mushrooms to make them soft

Take another bowl and tear chaffles down into minute pieces

Add the eggs and the veggies to it

Take a casserole dish, and add this new stuffing mixture to it

Bake it at 350 degrees for around 30 minutes and serve hot

## 28. Jalapeno Grilled Cheese Bacon Chaffle

Servings: 2

Preparation Time: 15 minutes

Total Time: 20 minutes

**What You Need:**

Egg: 2

Mozzarella Cheese: 1 cup (shredded)

Jalapenos: 2 sliced with seeds removed along with the skin

Cream cheese: ½ cup

Monterey jack: 2 slices

Cheddar cheese: 2 slices

Bacon: 4 slices cooked

**How To Cook:**

Add over two tablespoons of cream cheese to the half-cut jalapenos

Bake them for around 10 minutes and set aside

Preheat a mini waffle maker if needed and grease it

In a mixing bowl, beat eggs and add mozzarella cheese to them

Mix them all well

Pour the mixture to the lower plate of the waffle maker and spread it evenly to cover the plate properly

Close the lid

Cook for at least 4 minutes to get the desired crunch

Remove the chaffle from the heat and keep aside for around one minute

Make as many chaffles as your mixture and waffle maker allow

Make a sandwich by placing a slice of Monterey jack, a cheese slice, 2 bacon slice in between two chaffles and enjoy!

Servings: 2
Preparation Time: 5 minutes
Total Time: 10 minutes

**What You Need:**
Egg: 1
Mozzarella Cheese: 1/2 cup (shredded)
Bacon: 1 slice
Kewpie Mayo: 2 tbsp
Green onion: 1 stalk

**How To Cook:**
Preheat a mini waffle maker if needed and grease it
In a mixing bowl, beat an egg and put 1 tbsp of Kewpie Mayo
Chop green onion and put half of it in the mixing bowl and half aside
Cut bacon into pieces of ¼ inches and add in the mixing bowl

Mix them all well
Sprinkle around 1/8 cup of shredded mozzarella cheese to the lower plate of the waffle maker and pour the mixture over it
Again sprinkle 1/8 cup of shredded mozzarella cheese to the top of the mixture
Close the lid
Cook for at least 4 minutes to get the desired crunch
Remove the chaffle from the heat and drizzle Kewpie mayo
Serve by sprinkling the remaining green onions
Make as many chaffles as your mixture and waffle maker allow

Servings: 2
Preparation Time: 5 minutes
Total Time: 10 minutes
**What You Need:**
**For Chaffle:**
Egg: 2
Cream cheese: 2 tbsp
Vanilla extract: 1 tbsp
Almond flour: 2 tbsp
Heavy cream: 1 tsp
Cinnamon powder: 1 tsp
Swerve sweetener: 1 tbsp

**For Assembling:**
Cheese: 2 slices
Ham: 2 slices
Turkey: 2 slices

**How To Cook:**
Preheat a mini waffle maker if needed and grease it
In a mixing bowl, add all the chaffle ingredients
Mix them all well
Pour the mixture to the lower plate of the waffle maker and spread it evenly to cover the plate properly

Close the lid

Cook for at least 4 minutes to get the desired crunch

Remove the chaffle from the heat and keep aside for around one minute

Make as many chaffles as your mixture and waffle maker allow

Serve with a cheese slice, a turkey, and a ham

You can also serve with any of your favorite low carb raspberry jam on top

## 31. Zucchini Nut Bread Chaffle

Servings: 2
Preparation Time: 5 minutes
Total Time: 10 minutes

**What You Need:**
**For Chaffle:**
Egg: 1
Zucchini: 1 cup (shredded)
Cream Cheese: 2 tbsp softened
Cinnamon: 1/2 tsp
Erythritol blend: 1 tsp
Nutmeg: 1 tbsp (grounded)
Butter: 2 tsp
Baking powder: ½ tsp
Walnuts: 3 tbsp
Coconut flour: 2 tsp

**For Frosting:**
Cream cheese: 4 tbsp
Cinnamon: ¼ tsp
Butter: 2 tbsp
Caramel: 2 tbsp (sugar-free)
Walnuts: 1 tbsp (chopped)

**How To Cook:**
Grate zucchini and leave it in a colander for 10 minutes

Squeeze with your hands as well to drain much water

Preheat a mini waffle maker if needed and grease it

In a mixing bowl, beat an egg, zucchini, and other chaffle ingredients

Pour the mixture to the lower plate of the waffle maker and spread it evenly to cover the plate properly and close the lid

Cook for at least 4 minutes to get the desired crunch

Remove the chaffle from the heat

Make as many chaffles as your mixture and waffle maker allow

Whisk all the frosting ingredients together except for walnuts and give a uniform consistency

Serve the chaffles with frosting on top and chopped nuts

## 32. Garlic Bread Chaffle

Servings: 2
Preparation Time: 15 minutes
Total Time: 20 minutes

**What You Need:**
**For the Chaffle:**
Egg: 2
Mozzarella Cheese: 1 cup (shredded)
Garlic powder: ½ tsp
Italian seasoning: 1 tsp
Cream cheese: 1 tsp

**For the Garlic Butter Topping:**
Garlic powder: ½ tsp
Italian seasoning: 1/2 tsp
Butter: 1 tbsp
**For Cheesy Bread:**
Mozzarella Cheese: 2 tbsp (shredded)
Parsley: 1 tbsp

**How To Cook:**
Preheat a mini waffle maker if
needed and grease it

In a mixing bowl, add all the
ingredients of the chaffle and mix
well
Pour the mixture to the lower plate
of the waffle maker and spread it
evenly to cover the plate properly
and close the lid
Cook for at least 4 minutes to get the
desired crunch
In the meanwhile, melt butter and
add the garlic butter ingredients
Remove the chaffle from the heat
and apply the garlic butter
immediately
Make as many chaffles as your
mixture and waffle maker allow
Put the chaffles on the baking tray
and sprinkle the mozzarella cheese
on the chaffles
Bake for 5 minutes in an oven at 350
degrees to melt the cheese
Serve hot and enjoy

## 33. Peanut Butter & Jelly Sammich Chaffle

Servings: 2
Preparation Time: 20 minutes
Total Time: 30 minutes
**What You Need:**
**For Chaffle:**
Egg: 2
Mozzarella: ¼ cup
Vanilla extract: 1 tbsp
Coconut flour: 2 tbsp
Baking powder: ¼ tsp
Cinnamon powder: 1 tsp
Swerve sweetener: 1 tbsp
**For Blueberry Compote:**

Blueberries: 1 cup
Lemon zest: ½ tsp
Lemon juice: 1 tsp
Xanthan gum: 1/8 tsp
Water: 2 tbsp
Swerve sweetener: 1 tbsp
**How To Cook:**
For the blueberry compote, add all
the ingredients except xanthan gum
to a small pan
Mix them all and boil

Lower the heat and simmer for 8-10 minutes; the sauce will initiate to thicken

Add xanthan gum now and stir

Now remove the pan from the stove and allow the mixture to cool down

Put in refrigerator

Preheat a mini waffle maker if needed and grease it

In a mixing bowl, add all the chaffle ingredients and mix well

Pour the mixture to the lower plate of the waffle maker and spread it evenly to cover the plate properly

Close the lid

Cook for at least 4 minutes to get the desired crunch

Remove the chaffle from the heat and keep aside

Make as many chaffles as your mixture and waffle maker allow

Serve with the blueberry compote you prepared and enjoy!

## 34. Avocado Toast Chaffle

Servings: 2
Preparation Time: 5 minutes
Total Time: 10 minutes

**What You Need:**

Egg: 2
Cheddar cheese: 1 cup
Whole avocado: 1 whole
Lemon juice: 1 tsp
Salt: ¼ tsp or as per your taste
Black pepper: ¼ tsp or as per your taste

**How To Cook:**

Peel avocados, cut and put them in a bowl

Add salt, black pepper, and lemon juice to them

Mash them all together with the fork

Preheat a mini waffle maker if needed and grease it

In a mixing bowl, beat eggs and add cheddar cheese to them

Mix them all well and pour the mixture to the lower plate of the waffle maker

Close the lid

Cook for at least 4 minutes to get the desired crunch

Remove the chaffle from the heat and keep aside for around one minute

Apply the avocado spread to the chaffles and serve

Make as many chaffles as your mixture and waffle maker allow

## 35. Cinnamon Chaffle

Servings: 2
Preparation Time: 10 minutes
Total Time: 15 minutes

**What You Need:**

Egg: 1
Mozzarella: ½ cup
Vanilla extract: 1 tbsp
Almond flour: 1 tbsp
Baking powder: ½ tsp
Cinnamon powder: ½ tsp

**How To Cook:**

Preheat your waffle iron if needed
Mix all the above-mentioned ingredients in a bowl
Grease your waffle iron lightly
Cook in the waffle iron for about 5 minutes or till the desired crisp is achieved
Make as many chaffles as your mixture and waffle maker allow
Serve hot with your favorite toppings

## 36. Mc Griddle Chaffle

Servings: 2
Preparation Time: 5 minutes
Total Time: 10 minutes

**What You Need:**

Egg: 2
Mozzarella Cheese: 1½ cup (shredded)
Maple Syrup: 2 tbsp (sugar-free)
Sausage patty: 2
American cheese: 2 slices
Swerve/Monkfruit: 2 tbsp

**How To Cook:**

Preheat a mini waffle maker if needed and grease it
In a mixing bowl, beat eggs and add shredded mozzarella cheese, Swerve/Monkfruit, and maple syrup
Mix them all well and pour the mixture to the lower plate of the waffle maker

Close the lid
Cook for at least 4 minutes to get the desired crunch
Remove the chaffle from the heat
Prepare sausage patty by following the instruction given on the packaging
Place a cheese slice on the patty immediately when removing from heat
Take two chaffles and put sausage patty and cheese in between
Make as many chaffles as your mixture and waffle maker allow
Serve hot and enjoy!

## 37. Cinnamon Swirl Chaffle

Servings: 2
Preparation Time: 5 minutes
Total Time: 10 minutes

**What You Need:**
**For Chaffle:**
Egg: 2
Cream Cheese: 2 oz softened
Almond flour: 2 tbsp
Vanilla Extract: 2 tsp
Cinnamon: 2 tsp
Vanilla extract: 2 tsp
Splenda: 2 tbsp
**For Icing:**
Cream cheese: 2 oz softened

Splenda: 2 tbsp
Vanilla: 1 tsp
Butter: 2 tbsp unsalted butter
**For Cinnamon Drizzle:**
Splenda: 2 tbsp
Butter: 1 tbsp
Cinnamon: 2 tsp

**How To Cook:**
Preheat the waffle maker
Grease it lightly
Mix all the chaffle ingredients together
Pour the mixture to the waffle maker
Cook for around 4 minutes or till chaffles become crispy
Keep them aside when done
In a small bowl, mix the ingredients of icing and cinnamon drizzle

Heat it in a microwave for about 10 seconds to gain a soft uniformity
Whirl on cooled chaffles and enjoy!

## 38. Chicken Mozzarella Chaffle

Servings: 2
Preparation Time: 5 minutes
Total Time: 10 minutes

**What You Need:**
Chicken: 1 cup
Egg: 2
Mozzarella cheese: 1 cup and 4 tbsp
Tomato sauce: 6 tbsp
Basil: ½ tsp
Garlic: ½ tbsp
Butter: 1 tsp

**How To Cook:**
In a pan, add butter and include small pieces of chicken to it
Stir for two minutes and then add garlic and basil

Set aside the cooked chicken
Preheat the mini waffle maker if needed
Mix cooked chicken, eggs, and 1 cup mozzarella cheese properly

27

Spread it to the mini waffle maker thoroughly

Cook for 4 minutes or till it turns crispy and then remove it from the waffle maker

Make as many mini chaffles as you can

Now in a baking tray, line these mini chaffles and top with the tomato sauce and grated mozzarella cheese

Put the tray in the oven at 400 degrees until the cheese melts

Serve hot

## 39. Chicken Jamaican Jerk Chicken Chaffle

Servings: 2
Preparation Time: 15 minutes
Total Time: 30 minutes

**What You Need:**
**For Chaffle:**
Egg: 2
Mozzarella Cheese: 1 cup (shredded)
Butter: 1 tbsp
Almond flour: 2 tbsp
Turmeric: ¼ tsp
Baking powder: ¼ tsp
Xanthan gum: a pinch
Onion powder: a pinch
Garlic powder: a pinch
Salt: a pinch
**For Chicken Jamaican Jerk:**
Organic ground chicken: 1 pound
Dried thyme: 1 tsp
Garlic: 1 tsp (granulated)
Butter: 2 tbsp
Dried parsley: 2 tsp
Black pepper: 1/8 tsp
Salt: 1 tsp
Chicken broth: ½ cup
Jerk seasoning: 2 tbsp
Onion: ½ medium chopped

**How To Cook:**
In a pan, melt butter and sauté onion
Add all the remaining ingredients of chicken Jamaican jerk and sauté
Now add chicken and chicken broth and stir
Cook on medium-low heat for 10 minutes
Then cook on high heat and dry all the liquid
For chaffles, preheat a mini waffle maker if needed and grease it
In a mixing bowl, beat all the chaffle ingredients
Pour the mixture to the lower plate of the waffle maker and spread it evenly to cover the plate properly and close the lid
Cook for at least 4 minutes to get the desired crunch
Remove the chaffle from the heat and keep aside for around one minute
Make as many chaffles as your mixture and waffle maker allow
Add the chicken in between of a chaffle and fold and enjoy

## 40. Chicken Green Chaffles

Preparation time: 5 - 6 minutes

Servings: 4

Preparation Time: 10 minutes

Total Time: 15 minutes

**What You Need:**

**For Chaffle:**

Chicken: 1/3 cup boiled and shredded

Cabbage: 1/3 cup

Broccoli: 1/3 cup

Zucchini: 1/3 cup

Egg: 2

Mozzarella Cheese: 1 cup (shredded)

Butter: 1 tbsp

Almond flour: 2 tbsp

Baking powder: ¼ tsp

Onion powder: a pinch

Garlic powder: a pinch

Salt: a pinch

**How To Cook:**

In a deep saucepan, boil cabbage, broccoli, and zucchini for five minutes or till it tenders, strain, and blend

Mix all the remaining ingredients well together

Pour a thin layer on a preheated waffle iron

Add a layer of the blended vegetables on the mixture

Again add more mixture over the top

Cook the chaffle for around 5 minutes

Serve with your favorite sauce

## 41. Buffalo Chicken Chaffle

Servings: 2

Preparation Time: 5 minutes

Total Time: 10 minutes

**What You Need:**

Egg: 2

Cheddar Cheese: 1 cup

Buffalo sauce: 4 tbsp or as per your taste

Softened cream cheese: ¼ cup

Chicken: 1 cup

Butter: 1 tsp

**How To Cook:**

Heat the butter in the pan and add shredded chicken to it

Now remove from heat and add buffalo sauce as per your taste

In a bowl, add cooked chicken, cheddar cheese, softened cream cheese, and eggs

Mix all the ingredients well

Preheat the waffle maker and grease it

Now sprinkle a little cheddar cheese at the lower plate of the waffle maker

Spread your prepared batter evenly on the waffle maker

Now add a bit of cheese on the top as well and close the lid

Heat the chaffle for over 4 minutes or until it turns crispy

Make as many chaffles as your mixture and waffle maker allow

Serve hot with extra buffalo sauce

## 42. Artichoke and Spinach Chicken Chaffle

Servings: 2
Preparation Time: 10 minutes
Total Time: 25 minutes

**What You Need:**

Chicken: 1/3 cup cooked and diced
Spinach: 1/2 cup cooked and chopped
Artichokes: 1/3 cup chopped
Egg: 1
Mozzarella Cheese: 1/3 cup (shredded)
Cream cheese: 1 ounce
Garlic powder: ¼ tsp

**How To Cook:**

Preheat a mini waffle maker if needed and grease it

In a mixing bowl, add all the ingredients
Mix them all well
Pour the mixture to the lower plate of the waffle maker and spread it evenly to cover the plate properly
Close the lid
Cook for at least 4 minutes to get the desired crunch
Remove the chaffle from the heat and keep aside for around one minute
Make as many chaffles as your mixture and waffle maker allow
Serve hot and enjoy!

## 43. Garlic Chicken Chaffle

Servings: 2
Preparation Time: 10 minutes
Total Time: 25 minutes

**What You Need:**

Chicken: 3-4 pieces
Lemon juice: ½ tbsp
Garlic: 1 clove
Kewpie mayo: 2 tbsp
Egg: 1
Mozzarella cheese: ½ cup
Salt: As per your taste

**How To Cook:**

In a pot, cook the chicken by adding one cup of water to it with salt and bring to boil
Close the lid of the pot and cook for 15-20 minutes
When done, remove from stove and shred the chicken pieces leaving the bones behind; discard the bones

Grate garlic finely into pieces
Beat the egg in the mixing bowl, add garlic, lemon juice, Kewpie mayo, and 1/8 cup of cheese
Preheat the waffle maker if needed and grease it
Add the mixture to the waffle maker and cook for 4-5 minutes or until it is done
Remove the chaffles from the pan and preheat the oven
In the meanwhile, set the chaffles on a baking tray and spread the chicken on them
After that, sprinkle the remaining cheese on the chaffles
Put the tray in the oven and heat till the cheese melts
Serve hot
Make as many chaffles as you like

## 44. Chicken Cauli Chaffle

Servings: 2
Preparation Time: 12 minutes
Total Time: 25 minutes
**What You Need:**
Chicken: 3-4 pieces or ½ cup when done
Soy Sauce: 1 tbsp
Garlic: 2 clove
Cauliflower Rice: 1 cup
Egg: 2
Mozzarella cheese: 1 cup
Salt: As per your taste
Black pepper: ¼ tsp or as per your taste
White pepper: ¼ tsp or as per your taste
Green onion: 1 stalk
**How To Cook:**
Melt butter in oven or stove and set aside
In a pot, cook the chicken by adding one cup of water to it with salt and bring to boil
Close the lid of the pot and cook for 15-20 minutes

When done, remove from stove and shred the chicken pieces leaving the bones behind; discard the bones
Grate garlic finely into pieces
In a small bowl, beat egg and mix chicken, garlic, cauliflower rice, soy sauce, black pepper, and white pepper
Mix all the ingredients well
Preheat the waffle maker if needed and grease it
Place around 1/8 cup of shredded mozzarella cheese to the waffle maker
Pour the mixture over the cheese on the waffle maker and add 1/8 cup shredded cheese on top as well
Cook for 4-5 minutes or until it is done
Repeat and make as many chaffles as the batter can
Sprinkle chopped green onion on top and serve hot!

## 45. Easy Chicken Halloumi Burger Chaffle

Servings: 2
Preparation Time: 15 minutes
Total Time: 20 minutes

**What You Need:**
**For the Chaffle:**
Egg: 2
Mozzarella Cheese: 1 cup (shredded)
Butter: 1 tbsp
Almond flour: 2 tbsp
Baking powder: ¼ tsp

Onion powder: a pinch

Garlic powder: a pinch
Salt: a pinch
**For the Chicken Patty:**
Ground chicken: 1 lb
Onion powder: ½ tbsp
Garlic powder: ½ tbsp
Halloumi cheese: 1 cup
Salt: ¼ tsp or as per your taste
Black pepper: ¼ tsp or as per your taste

**For Serving:**

Lettuce leaves: 2

American cheese: 2 slices

**How To Cook:**

Mix all the chicken patty ingredient in a bowl

Make equal-sized patties; either grill them or fry them

Preheat a mini waffle maker if needed and grease it

In a mixing bowl, add all the chaffle ingredients and mix well

Pour the mixture to the lower plate of the waffle maker and spread it evenly to cover the plate properly and close the lid

Cook for at least 4 minutes to get the desired crunch

Remove the chaffle from the heat and keep aside for around one minute

Make as many chaffles as your mixture and waffle maker allow

Serve with the chicken patties, lettuce, and a cheese slice in between of two chaffles

## 46. Chicken Eggplant Chaffle

Servings: 2

Preparation Time: 15 minutes

Total Time: 25 minutes

**What You Need:**

**For Chaffles:**

Eggs: 2

Cheddar cheese: ½ cup

Parmesan cheese: 2 tbsp

Italian season: ¼ tsp

Chicken: 1 cup

**For Eggplant:**

Eggplant: 1 big

Salt: 1 pinch

Black pepper: 1 pinch

**How To Cook:**

Boil the chicken in water for 15 minutes and strain

Shred the chicken into small pieces and set aside

ut the eggplant in slices and boil in water and strain

Add a pinch of salt and pepper

Add all the chaffle ingredients in a bowl and mix well to make a mixture

Add the boiled chicken as well

Preheat a mini waffle maker if needed and grease it

Pour the mixture to the lower plate of the waffle maker and spread it evenly to cover the plate properly

Add the eggplant over two slices on the mixture and cover the lid

Cook for at least 4 minutes to get the desired crunch

Remove the chaffle from the heat and keep aside for around one minute

Make as many chaffles as your mixture and waffle maker allow

Serve hot with your favorite sauce

## 47. Chicken Garlic Chaffle Roll

Preparation time: 10 - 12 minutes
Servings: 2
Preparation Time: 20 minutes
Total Time: 30 minutes

**What You Need:**

Chicken mince: 1 cup
Salt: ¼ tsp or as per your taste
Black pepper: ¼ tsp or as per your taste
Egg: 2
Lemon juice: 1 tbsp
Mozzarella Cheese: 1 cup (shredded)
Butter: 2 tbsp
Garlic powder: 1½ tsp
Bay seasoning: ½ tsp
Parsley: for garnishing

**How To Cook:**

In a frying pan, melt butter and add chicken mince
When done, add salt, pepper, 1 tbsp garlic powder, and lemon juice and set aside
In a mixing bowl, beat eggs and add mozzarella cheese to them with ½ garlic powder and bay seasoning
Mix them all well and pour to the greasy mini waffle maker
Cook for at least 4 minutes to get the desired crunch
Remove the chaffle from the heat, add the chicken mixture in between and fold
Make as many chaffles as your mixture and waffle maker allow
Top with parsley
Serve hot and enjoy!

## 48. Ginger Chicken Cucumber Chaffle Roll

Servings: 2
Preparation Time: 20 minutes
Total Time: 30 minutes

**What You Need:**
**For Garlic Chicken:**

Chicken mince: 1 cup
Salt: ¼ tsp or as per your taste
Black pepper: ¼ tsp or as per your taste
Lemon juice: 1 tbsp
Butter: 2 tbsp
Garlic juvenile: 2 tbsp
Garlic powder: 1 tsp
Soy sauce: 1 tbsp

**For Chaffle:**
Egg: 2
Mozzarella cheese: 1 cup (shredded)
Garlic powder: 1 tsp
**For Serving:**
Cucumber: ½ cup (diced)
Parsley: 1 tbsp

**How To Cook:**

In a frying pan, melt butter and add juvenile garlic and sauté for 1 minute
Now add chicken mince and cook till it tenders

When done, add rest of the ingredients and set aside

In a mixing bowl, beat eggs and add mozzarella cheese to them with garlic powder

Mix them all well and pour to the greasy mini waffle maker

Cook for at least 4 minutes to get the desired crunch

Remove the chaffle from the heat, add the chicken mixture in between with cucumber and fold

Make as many chaffles as your mixture and waffle maker allow

Serve hot and top with parsley

## 49. Chinese Chicken Chaffle

Servings: 2
Preparation Time: 20 minutes
Total Time: 30 minutes

**What You Need:**
**For the Chaffle:**
Egg: 2
Mozzarella Cheese: 1 cup (shredded)
Butter: 1 tbsp
Almond flour: 2 tbsp
Baking powder: ¼ tsp
Salt: a pinch
**For the Chicken:**
Chicken pieces: 2-4
Ginger powder: ½ tbsp
Salt: ¼ tsp or as per your taste
Black pepper: ¼ tsp or as per your taste
Soy sauce: 1 tbsp
Spring onion: 1 stalk

**How To Cook:**
Boil the chicken in saucepan, when done remove from water and pat dry

Shred the chicken into small pieces and add all the seasoning and spices

Finely chop the spring onion and mix with the chicken and set aside

Preheat a mini waffle maker if needed and grease it

In a mixing bowl, add all the chaffle ingredients and mix well

Pour a little amount of mixture to the lower plate of the waffle maker and spread it evenly to cover the plate properly

Add the chicken mixture on top and again spread the thin layer of mixture and close the lid

Cook for at least 4 minutes to get the desired crunch

Remove the chaffle from the heat

Make as many chaffles as your mixture and waffle maker allow

Serve hot and enjoy

# 50. Chicken Jalapeno Chaffle

Servings: 2
Preparation Time: 15 minutes
Total Time: 25 minutes

**What You Need:**
Egg: 2
Cheddar cheese: 1½ cup
Deli Jalapeno: 16 slices
Boiled chicken: 1 cup (shredded)

**How To Cook:**
Preheat a mini waffle maker if needed
In a mixing bowl, beat eggs and add chicken and half cheddar cheese to them
Mix them all well
Shred some of the remaining cheddar cheese to the lower plate of the waffle maker
Now pour the mixture to the shredded cheese
Add the cheese again on the top with around 4 slices of jalapeno and close the lid
Cook for at least 4 minutes to get the desired crunch
Serve hot
Make as many chaffles as your mixture allows

# 51. Chicken Stuffed Chaffles

Servings: 2
Preparation Time: 15 minutes
Total Time: 40 minutes

**What You Need:**
**For Chaffle:**
Egg: 2
Mozzarella Cheese: ½ cup (shredded)
Garlic powder: ¼ tsp
Salt: ¼ tsp or as per your taste
Black pepper: ¼ tsp or as per your taste
**For Stuffing:**
Onion: 1 small diced
Chicken: 1 cup
Butter: 4 tbsp
Salt: ¼ tsp or as per your taste
Black pepper: ¼ tsp or as per your taste

**How To Cook:**
Preheat a mini waffle maker if needed and grease it
In a mixing bowl, add all the chaffle ingredients
Mix them all well
Pour the mixture to the lower plate of the waffle maker and spread it evenly to cover the plate properly and close the lid
Cook for at least 4 minutes to get the desired crunch
Remove the chaffle from the heat and keep aside
Make as many chaffles as your mixture and waffle maker allow
Take a small frying pan and melt butter in it on medium-low heat
Sauté chicken and onion and add salt and pepper
Take another bowl and tear chaffles down into minute pieces
Add chicken and onion to it
Take a casserole dish, and add this new stuffing mixture to it
Bake it at 350 degrees for around 30 minutes and serve hot

## 52. Easy Chicken Vegetable Chaffles

Servings: 2
Preparation Time: 20 minutes
Total Time: 30 minutes
**What You Need:**
**For the Chaffle:**
Egg: 2
Mozzarella Cheese: 1 cup (shredded)
Salt: a pinch

**For the Chicken:**
Chicken pieces: 2-4
Ginger powder: ½ tbsp
Salt: ¼ tsp or as per your taste
Black pepper: ¼ tsp or as per your taste
Cauliflower: 3 tbsp
Cabbage: 3 tbsp
Green pepper: 1 tbsp
Spring onion: 1 stalk

**How To Cook:**
Boil the chicken, green pepper, cauliflower, and cabbage in saucepan, when done strain the water

Shred the chicken into small pieces and blend all the vegetables and mix them together

Finely chop the spring onion and mix with the chicken and set aside

Preheat a mini waffle maker if needed and grease it

In a mixing bowl, add all the chaffle ingredients and mix well

Pour a little amount of mixture to the lower plate of the waffle maker and spread it evenly to cover the plate properly

Add the chicken mixture on top and again spread the thin layer of mixture and close the lid

Cook for at least 4 minutes to get the desired crunch

Remove the chaffle from the heat

Make as many chaffles as your mixture and waffle maker allow

Serve hot and enjoy

## 53. Roasted Cabbage Chicken Chaffle

Servings: 2
Preparation Time: 12 minutes
Total Time: 25 minutes

**What You Need:**
Chicken: 3-4 pieces or ½ cup when done
Soy Sauce: 1 tbsp
Garlic: 2 clove
Cabbage: 1 cup
Egg: 2
Mozzarella cheese: 1 cup
Salt: As per your taste
Black pepper: ¼ tsp or as per your taste
White pepper: ¼ tsp or as per your taste

**How To Cook:**
Melt butter in oven or stove and set aside

In a pot, cook the chicken and cabbage by adding one cup of water to it with salt and bring to boil

Close the lid of the pot and cook for 15-20 minutes

When done, remove from stove and shred the chicken pieces leaving the bones behind; discard the bones

Strain water from cabbage and blend

Grate garlic finely into pieces

In a small bowl, beat egg and mix chicken, cabbage, garlic, soy sauce, black pepper, and white pepper

36

Mix all the ingredients well

Preheat the waffle maker if needed and grease it

Place around 1/8 cup of shredded mozzarella cheese to the waffle maker

Pour the mixture over the cheese on the waffle maker and add 1/8 cup shredded cheese on top as well

Cook for 4-5 minutes or until it is done

Make as many chaffles as your mixture and waffle maker allow

Serve hot!

## 54. Chicken Zucchini Chaffle

Servings: 2
Preparation Time: 12 minutes
Total Time: 25 minutes
**What You Need:**

Chicken: 1 cup boneless pieces
Zucchini: 1 (small)
Egg: 2
Salt: as per your taste
Shredded mozzarella: 1 cup
Parmesan: 2 tbsp
Pepper: as per your taste
Basil: 1 tsp
Water: ½ cup

**How To Cook:**

In a small saucepan, add chicken with a half cup of water and boil till chicken tenders

Preheat your waffle iron

Grate zucchini finely

Add all the ingredients to zucchini in a bowl and mix well

Shred chicken finely and add it as well

Grease your waffle iron lightly

Pour the mixture into a full-size waffle maker and spread evenly

Cook till it turns crispy

Make as many chaffles as your mixture and waffle maker allow

Serve crispy and hot

## 55. Chicken Spinach Chaffle

Servings: 2
Preparation Time: 10 minutes
Total Time: 40 minutes

**What You Need:**

Spinach: ½ cup
Chicken: ½ cup boneless
Egg: 1
Shredded mozzarella: half cup
Pepper: As per your taste
Garlic powder: 1 tbsp
Onion powder: 1 tbsp
Salt: As per your taste
Basil: 1 tsp

**How To Cook:**

Boil chicken in water to make it tender

Shred-it into small pieces and set aside

Boil spinach in a saucepan for 10 minutes and strain

Preheat your waffle iron

Add all the ingredients to boiled spinach in a bowl and mix well

Now add the shredded chicken

Grease your waffle iron lightly

Pour the mixture into a full-size waffle maker and spread evenly

Cook till it turns crispy

Make as many chaffles as your mixture and waffle maker allow

Serve crispy and with your favorite keto sauce

## 56. Chicken BBQ Chaffle

Servings: 2
Preparation Time: 10 minutes
Total Time: 30 minutes

**What You Need**:

Chicken: 1/2 cup
Butter: 1 tbsp
BBQ sauce: 1 tbsp (sugar-free)
Almond flour: 2 tbsp
Egg: 1
Cheddar cheese: ½ cup

**How To Cook:**

Cook the chicken in the butter on a low-medium heat for 10 minutes
Preheat your waffle iron

In mixing bowl, add all the chaffle ingredients including chicken and mix well

Grease your waffle iron lightly

Pour the mixture to the bottom plate evenly; also spread it out to get better results and close the upper plate and heat

Cook for 6 minutes or until the chaffle is done

Make as many chaffles as your mixture and waffle maker allow

## 57. Crispy Fried Chicken Chaffle

Servings: 2
Preparation Time: 25 minutes
Total Time: 45 minutes

**What You Need:**
**For Chaffle:**
Egg: 1
Mozzarella Cheese: ½ cup (shredded)
**For Fried Chicken:**
Chicken strips: 8 pieces
Butter: 2 tbsp
Salt: ¼ tsp or as per your taste
Black pepper: ¼ tsp or as per your taste
Red chili flakes: ½ tsp
**How To Cook:**

In a frying pan, melt butter and fry chicken strips on medium-low heat
Add the spices at the end and set aside
Mix all the chaffle ingredients well together
Pour a thin layer on a preheated waffle iron
Add chicken strips and pour again more mixture over the top
Cook the chaffle for around 5 minutes
Make as many chaffles as your mixture and waffle maker allow
Serve hot!

## 58. Jalapeno Chicken Popper Chaffle

Servings: 2
Preparation Time: 25 minutes
Total Time: 45 minutes

**What You Need:**
Canned chicken breast: ½ cup
Onion powder: 1/8 tsp
Garlic powder: 1/8 tsp
Eggs: 1
Cheddar cheese: 1/4 cup
Jalapeno: 1 diced
Cream cheese: 1 tbsp
Parmesan cheese: 1/8 tbsp

**How To Cook:**
Preheat a mini waffle maker if needed and grease it
In a mixing bowl, beat eggs and add all the ingredients
Mix them all well
Pour the mixture to the lower plate of the waffle maker and spread it evenly to cover the plate properly
Close the lid
Cook for at least 4 minutes to get the desired crunch
Remove the chaffle from the heat and keep aside for around one minute
Make as many chaffles as your mixture and waffle maker allow
Serve hot and enjoy!

Preparation Time: 15 minutes

Total Time: 30 minutes

**What You Need:**

**For Chaffle:**

Egg: 2

Mozzarella cheese: 1 cup (shredded)

Avocado: half

Green Leaf Lettuce: 2 leaves optional

**For Patty:**

Ground Beef: ½ lb

Pork Panko: 1 tbsp

Salt: ¼ tsp

Egg: 1

Salt: ¼ tsp or as per your taste

Black pepper: ¼ tsp or as per your taste

**For Teriyaki Sauce:**

Japanese Sake: 2 tbsp

Soy Sauce: 1 tbsp

Xanthan Gum: 1/8 tsp

Swerve/Monkfruit: 1 tbsp

**How To Cook:**

In a saucepan, add Japanese Sake, Soy Sauce, Xanthan Gum, and Swerve/Monkfruit and bring to boil on high heat

Then lower the heat and cook the mixture for a minute or two and mix continuously

When Xanthan Gum dissolves, remove from heat and let it cool

Take a mixing bowl and add ground beef, pork panko, egg, salt, and pepper, and mix with your hands

When the mixture becomes smooth, turn it into a ball and press it on a plate and make it a patty

A patty should be over ¼ inch thick and make sure to put your thumb in between the patty so that it doesn't expand upward and retains its shape

Preheat the grill to 350 degrees and cook the patties from both sides on medium to low heat for 4-5 minutes till patties turn brown

You can also use a frying pan to fry the patties

Preheat a mini waffle maker if needed

In a mixing bowl, beat eggs and add mozzarella cheese to them

Mix them all well and pour to the greasy mini waffle maker

Cook for at least 4 minutes to get the desired crunch

Remove the chaffle from the heat and keep aside

Make as many chaffles as your mixture and waffle maker allow

Cut avocado in slices

Wash green leaf lettuce and dry

Take two chaffles and arrange a beef patty with the slices of avocado, green lettuce, and teriyaki sauce in between to make a burger

Serve hot and enjoy

## 60. Sloppy Joe Chaffle

Servings: 2
Preparation Time: 15 minutes
Total Time: 30 minutes

**What You Need:**
**For Sloppy Joe:**
Ground beef: 1 lb
Onion powder: 1 tsp
Tomato paste: 3 tbsp
Garlic: 1 tsp (minced)
Chili powder: 1 tbsp
Cocoa powder: 1 tbsp
Bone broth: ½ cup
Coconut aminos: 1 tsp (soy sauce could be used instead)
Mustard powder: 1 tbsp
Paprika: ½ tsp
Swerve brown: 1 tsp
Salt: ¼ tsp or as per your taste
Black pepper: ¼ tsp or as per your taste
**For Cornbread Chaffle:**
Egg: 1
Cheddar cheese: ½ cup
Jalapeno: 5 slices (diced)
Corn extract: ¼ tsp
Salt: ¼ tsp or as per your taste

Franks red hot sauce: 1 tsp
**How To Cook:**
In a saucepan, add ground beef and sprinkle salt and pepper first
Now add all the other ingredients and let it simmer
Preheat a mini waffle maker if needed and grease it
In a mixing bowl, beat eggs and add cheddar cheese to them with the remaining ingredients
Pour the mixture to the lower plate of the waffle maker and spread it evenly to cover the plate properly and close the lid
Cook for at least 4 minutes to get the desired crunch
Remove the chaffle from the heat
Make as many chaffles as your mixture and waffle maker allow
Add the warm Sloppy Joe on top
Serve hot and enjoy!

## 61 Beef Strips Chaffle

Servings: 2
Preparation Time: 25 minutes
Total Time: 45 minutes
**What You Need:**
**For Chaffle:**
Egg: 1
Mozzarella Cheese: ½ cup (shredded)
Salt: ¼ tsp or as per your taste
Black pepper: ¼ tsp or as per your taste
Ginger powder: 1 tbsp

**For Beef Strips:**
Beef strips: 8 pieces
Butter: 2 tbsp
Salt: ¼ tsp or as per your taste
Black pepper: ¼ tsp or as per your taste
Red chili flakes: ½ tsp
**How To Cook:**
In a frying pan, melt butter and fry beef strips on medium-low heat

Add water to make them tender and boil for 30 minutes

Add the spices at the end and set aside

Mix all the chaffle ingredients well together

Pour a thin layer on a preheated waffle iron

Add beef strips and pour again more mixture over the top

Cook the chaffle for around 5 minutes

Make as many chaffles as your mixture and waffle maker allow

Serve hot with your favorite sauce

## 62. Beef BBQ Chaffle

Servings: 2
Preparation Time: 10 minutes
Total Time: 40 minutes

**What You Need:**
Beef mince: 1/2 cup
Butter: 1 tbsp
BBQ sauce: 1 tbsp (sugar-free)
Almond flour: 2 tbsp
Egg: 1
Cheddar cheese: ½ cup

**How To Cook:**
Cook the beef mince in the butter and half cup water on a low-medium heat for 20 minutes

Then increase the flame to reduce water

Preheat your waffle iron

In mixing bowl, add all the chaffle ingredients including beef mince and mix well

Grease your waffle iron lightly

Pour the mixture to the bottom plate evenly; also spread it out to get better results and close the upper plate and heat

Cook for 6 minutes or until the chaffle is done

Make as many chaffles as your mixture and waffle maker allow

## 63. .Beef Eggplant Chaffle

Servings: 2
Preparation Time: 15 minutes
Total Time: 45 minutes

**What You Need:**
**For Chaffles:**
Eggs: 2
Cheddar cheese: ½ cup
Parmesan cheese: 2 tbsp
Italian season: ¼ tsp
Beef mince: 1 cup
**For Eggplant:**

Eggplant: 1 big
Salt: 1 pinch
Black pepper: 1 pinch
Red chili flakes: 1/2 tsp

**How To Cook:**
Cook the beef mince with half cup water on medium-low flame for 20 minutes

Increase the flame afterward to remove excess water

Cut the eggplant in slices and boil in water and strain

Add a pinch of salt and pepper with red chili flakes

Add all the chaffle ingredients in a bowl and mix well to make a mixture

Add the boiled beef

Preheat a mini waffle maker if needed and grease it

Pour the mixture to the lower plate of the waffle maker and spread it evenly to cover the plate properly

Add the eggplant about two slices on the mixture and cover the lid

Cook for at least 4 minutes to get the desired crunch

Remove the chaffle from the heat

Make as many chaffles as your mixture and waffle maker allow

Serve hot with your favorite sauce

## 64. Beef Stuffed Chaffles

Servings: 2
Preparation Time: 15 minutes
Total Time: 50 minutes

**What You Need:**
**For Chaffle:**
Egg: 2
Mozzarella Cheese: ½ cup (shredded)
Garlic powder: ¼ tsp
Salt: ¼ tsp or as per your taste
Black pepper: ¼ tsp or as per your taste
**For Stuffing:**
Onion: 1 small diced
Beef mince: 1 cup
Butter: 4 tbsp
Salt: ¼ tsp or as per your taste

Black pepper: ¼ tsp or as per your taste

**How To Cook:**
Preheat a mini waffle maker if needed and grease it
In a mixing bowl, add all the chaffle ingredients
Mix them all well

Pour the mixture to the lower plate of the waffle maker and spread it evenly to cover the plate properly and close the lid

Cook for at least 4 minutes to get the desired crunch

Remove the chaffle from the heat and keep aside

Make as many chaffles as your mixture and waffle maker allow

Take a small frying pan and melt butter in it on medium-low heat

Sauté beef mince and onion and add salt and pepper

Cook for over 20 minutes

Take another bowl and tear chaffles down into minute pieces

Add beef and onion to it

Take a casserole dish, and add this new stuffing mixture to it

Bake it at 350 degrees for around 30 minutes and serve hot

## 65. Jalapeno Beef Chaffle

Servings: 2
Preparation Time: 25 minutes
Total Time: 45 minutes

**What You Need:**
Boiled Beef: ½ cup shredded
Onion powder: 1/8 tsp
Garlic powder: 1/8 tsp
Eggs: 1
Cheddar cheese: 1/4 cup
Jalapeno: 1 diced
Cream cheese: 1 tbsp
Parmesan cheese: 1/8 tbsp

**How To Cook:**
Preheat a mini waffle maker if needed and grease it

In a mixing bowl, beat an egg and add all the ingredients
Mix them all well
Pour the mixture to the lower plate of the waffle maker and spread it evenly to cover the plate properly
Close the lid
Cook for at least 4 minutes to get the desired crunch
Remove the chaffle from the heat and keep aside for around one minute
Make as many chaffles as your mixture and waffle maker allow
Serve hot and enjoy!

## 66. Beef Pickled Sandwich Chaffle

Servings: 2
Preparation Time: 20 minutes
Total Time: 1 hour 30 minutes

**What You Need:**
**For Beef:**
Chicken Breast: 1
Parmesan cheese: 4 tbsp
Dill pickle juice: 4 tbsp
Pork rinds: 2 tbsp
Flaxseed: 1 tsp (grounded)
Butter: 1 tsp
Salt: ¼ tsp or as per your taste
Black pepper: ¼ tsp or as per your taste
**For Sandwich Bun:**
Egg: 1
Mozzarella Cheese: 1 cup (shredded)
Stevia glycerite: 4 drops
Butter extract: ¼ tsp

**How To Cook:**
Cut the beef into half-inch pieces and add in a ziplock bag with pickle juice
Keep them together for an hour to overnight
In a mixing bowl add all the beef ingredients and mix well
Now add the beef and discard the pickle juice
Cook the beef on the frying pan for 6 minutes from each side at low flame and set aside
Mix all the sandwich bun ingredients in a bowl
Put the mixture to the mini waffle maker and cook for 4 minutes
Remove from heat
Make the chaffle sandwich by adding the prepared beef in between

## 67. Ginger Beef Chaffle

Servings: 2
Preparation Time: 20 minutes
Total Time: 40 minutes

**What You Need:**
**For Garlic Beef:**
Beef mince: 1 cup
Salt: ¼ tsp or as per your taste
Black pepper: ¼ tsp or as per your taste
Butter: 2 tbsp
Garlic juvenile: 2 tbsp
Garlic powder: 1 tsp
Soy sauce: 1 tbsp
Water: ½ cup

**For Chaffle:**
Egg: 2
Mozzarella cheese: 1 cup (shredded)
Garlic powder: 1 tsp

**How To Cook:**

In a frying pan, melt butter and add juvenile garlic and sauté for 1 minute

Now add beef mince and cook by adding water till it tenders

Let the water to dry out, when done, add rest of the ingredients and set aside

In a mixing bowl, beat eggs and add mozzarella cheese to them with garlic powder

Mix them all well and pour to the greasy mini waffle maker

Cook for at least 4 minutes to get the desired crunch

Remove the chaffle from the heat and top with garlic beef

Make as many chaffles as your mixture and waffle maker allow

Serve hot and enjoy

## 68. Easy Beef Burger Chaffle

Servings: 2
Preparation Time: 20 minutes
Total Time: 30 minutes

**What You Need:**
**For the Chaffle:**
Egg: 2
Mozzarella Cheese: 1 cup (shredded)
Butter: 1 tbsp
Almond flour: 2 tbsp
Baking powder: ¼ tsp
Salt: a pinch

**For the Beef Patty:**
Ground beef: 1 lb
Onion powder: ½ tbsp
Garlic powder: ½ tbsp
Red chili flakes: ½ tbsp
Cheddar cheese: 1 cup
Salt: ¼ tsp or as per your taste

Black pepper: ¼ tsp or as per your taste

**For Serving:**
Lettuce leaves: 2
American cheese: 2 slices

**How To Cook:**

Mix all the beef patty ingredient in a bowl

Make equal-sized patties; either grill them or fry them on a medium-low heat

Preheat a mini waffle maker if needed and grease it

In a mixing bowl, add all the chaffle ingredients and mix well

Pour the mixture to the lower plate of the waffle maker and spread it evenly to cover the plate properly and close the lid

Cook for at least 4 minutes to get the desired crunch

Remove the chaffle from the heat and keep aside for around one minute

Make as many chaffles as your mixture and waffle maker allow

Serve with the beef patties, lettuce, and a cheese slice in between of two chaffles

## 69. Beef Garlic Chaffle Roll

Servings: 2
Preparation Time: 20 minutes
Total Time: 40 minutes

**What You Need:**
Beef mince: 1 cup
Salt: ¼ tsp or as per your taste
Black pepper: ¼ tsp or as per your taste
Egg: 2
Lemon juice: 1 tbsp
Water: 1/2 cup
Mozzarella Cheese: 1 cup (shredded)
Butter: 2 tbsp
Garlic powder: 1½ tsp

Bay seasoning: ½ tsp
Parsley: for garnishing
Cabbage: ½ cup

**How To Cook:**
In a frying pan, melt butter and add the beef mince

Add ½ cup water for the mince to tender

When done, add salt, pepper, 1 tbsp garlic powder, and lemon juice and set aside

In a mixing bowl, beat eggs and add mozzarella cheese to them with ½ garlic powder and bay seasoning

Mix them all well and pour to the greasy mini waffle maker

Cook for at least 4 minutes to get the desired crunch

Remove the chaffle from the heat, add the beef mixture in between and fold

Make as many chaffles as your mixture and waffle maker allow

Top with parsley and add cabbage in between

Serve hot and enjoy!

## 70. Cauli Beef Chaffle

Servings: 2
Preparation Time: 20 minutes
Total Time: 45 minutes

**What You Need:**

Beef fine mince: 1 cup
Soy Sauce: 1 tbsp
Garlic: 2 clove
Cauliflower rice: 1 cup
Egg: 2
Mozzarella cheese: 1 cup
Salt: As per your taste
Black pepper: ¼ tsp or as per your taste
White pepper: ¼ tsp or as per your taste
Green onion: 1 stalk

**How To Cook:**

Melt butter in oven or stove and set aside
In a pot, cook the beef mince by adding one cup of water to it with salt and bring to boil
Close the lid of the pot and cook for 15-20 minutes
When done, cook on high flame till the water dries
Grate garlic finely into pieces
In a small bowl, beat egg and mix the beef mince, garlic, cauliflower rice, soy sauce, black pepper, and white pepper
Mix all the ingredients well
Preheat the waffle maker if needed and grease it
Place around 1/8 cup of shredded mozzarella cheese to the waffle maker
Pour the mixture over the cheese on the waffle maker and add 1/8 cup shredded cheese on top as well
Cook for 4-5 minutes or until it is done
Repeat and make as many chaffles as the batter can
Sprinkle chopped green onion on top and serve hot!

## 71. Beef Zucchini Chaffle

Servings: 2
Preparation Time: 10 minutes
Total Time: 45 minutes

**What You Need:**

Zucchini: 1 (small)
Beef: ½ cup boneless
Egg: 1
Shredded mozzarella: half cup
Pepper: As per your taste
Salt: As per your taste
Basil: 1 tsp

**How To Cook:**

Boil beef in water to make it tender

Shred it into small pieces and set aside

Preheat your waffle iron

Grate zucchini finely

Add all the ingredients to zucchini in a bowl and mix well

Now add the shredded beef

Grease your waffle iron lightly

Pour the mixture into a full-size waffle maker and spread evenly

Cook till it turns crispy

Make as many chaffles as your mixture and waffle maker allow

Serve crispy and with your favorite keto sauce

## 72. Spinach Beef Chaffle

Servings: 2
Preparation Time: 10 minutes
Total Time: 45 minutes

**What You Need:**

Spinach: ½ cup

Beef: ½ cup boneless

Egg: 1

Shredded mozzarella: half cup

Pepper: As per your taste

Garlic powder: 1 tbsp

Salt: As per your taste

Basil: 1 tsp

**How To Cook:**

Boil beef in water to make it tender

Shred it into small pieces and set aside

Boil spinach in a saucepan for 10 minutes and strain

Preheat your waffle iron

Add all the ingredients to boiled spinach in a bowl and mix well

Now add the shredded beef

Grease your waffle iron lightly

Pour the mixture into a full-size waffle maker and spread evenly

Cook till it turns crispy

Make as many chaffles as your mixture and waffle maker allow

Serve crispy and with your favorite keto sauce)

## 73. Crispy Beef Burger Chaffle

Servings: 2
Preparation Time: 20 minutes
Total Time: 50 minutes

**What You Need:**
**For the Chaffle:**
Egg: 2
Mozzarella Cheese: 1 cup (shredded)
Butter: 1 tbsp
Almond flour: 2 tbsp
Baking powder: ¼ tsp
Onion powder: a pinch
Garlic powder: a pinch
Salt: a pinch
**For the Beef:**
Ground beef: 1 lb
Chives: 2 tbsp
Cheddar cheese: 1 cup
Salt: ¼ tsp or as per your taste
Black pepper: ¼ tsp or as per your taste

**How To Cook:**
Mix all the beef ingredient in a bowl
Make patties either grill them or fry them
Preheat a mini waffle maker if needed and grease it
In a mixing bowl, add all the chaffle ingredients and mix well
Pour the mixture to the lower plate of the waffle maker and spread it evenly to cover the plate properly and close the lid
Cook for at least 4 minutes to get the desired crunch
Remove the chaffle from the heat and keep aside for around one minute
Make as many chaffles as your mixture and waffle maker allow
Serve with the beef patties in between two chaffles

## 74. Crispy Beef Artichoke Chaffle

Servings: 2
Preparation Time: 10 minutes
Total Time: 40 minutes

**What You Need:**
Beef: ½ cup cooked grounded
Artichokes: 1 cup chopped
Egg: 1
Mozzarella Cheese: 1/2 cup (shredded)
Cream cheese: 1 ounce
Salt: as per your taste
Garlic powder: ¼ tsp
Onion powder: ¼ tsp

**How To Cook:**
Preheat a mini waffle maker if needed and grease it

In a mixing bowl, add all the ingredients
Mix them all well
Pour the mixture to the lower plate of the waffle maker and spread it evenly to cover the plate properly
Close the lid
Cook for at least 4 minutes to get the desired crunch
Remove the chaffle from the heat and keep aside for around one minute
Make as many chaffles as your mixture and waffle maker allow
Serve hot with your favorite keto sauce

49

## 75. Beef Cheddar Chaffle

Servings: 2
Preparation Time: 15 minutes
Total Time: 45 minutes

**What You Need:**
Beef: 1 cup (grounder)
Egg: 2
Chedder cheese: 1 cup
Mozarrella cheese: 4 tbsp
Tomato sauce: 6 tbsp
Basil: ½ tsp
Garlic: ½ tbsp
Butter: 1 tsp

**How To Cook:**
In a pan, add butter and include beef
Stir for two minutes and then add garlic and basil
Cook till tender
Set aside the cooked beef
Preheat the mini waffle maker if needed
Mix cooked beef, eggs, and 1 cup mozzarella cheese properly
Spread it to the mini waffle maker thoroughly
Cook for 4 minutes or till it turns crispy and then remove it from the waffle maker
Make as many mini chaffles as you can
Now in a baking tray, line these mini chaffles and top with the tomato sauce and grated mozzarella cheese
Put the tray in the oven at 400 degrees until the cheese melts
Serve hot with your favorite keto sauce
.

## 76. Beef Broccoli Chaffle

Servings: 2
Preparation Time: 10 minutes
Total Time: 45 minutes
**What You Need:**
Broccoli: ½ cup
Beef: ½ cup boneless
Butter: 2 tbsp
Egg: 1
Shredded mozzarella: half cup
Pepper: As per your taste
Garlic powder: 1 tbsp
Salt: As per your taste
Basil: 1 tsp
**How To Cook:**
In a pan, add butter and include beef
Stir for two minutes and then add garlic and basil
Cook till tender
Boil broccoli for 10 minutes in a separate pan and blend
Set aside the cooked beef
Preheat the mini waffle maker if needed
Mix cooked beef, broccoli blend, eggs, and 1 cup mozzarella cheese properly
Spread it to the mini waffle maker thoroughly
Cook for 4 minutes or till it turns crispy and then remove it from the waffle maker
Make as many mini chaffles as you can
Now in a baking tray, line these mini chaffles and top with the tomato sauce and grated mozzarella cheese
Put the tray in the oven at 400 degrees until the cheese melts
Serve hot with your favorite keto sauce

# SEAFOOD CHAFFLES

## 77. Crab Chaffle Roll

Servings: 2
Preparation Time: 5 minutes
Total Time: 10 minutes

**What You Need:**
Crab Meat: 1 ½ cup
Egg: 2
Mozzarella Cheese: 1 cup (shredded)
Lemon juice: 2 tsp
Kewpie Mayo: 2 tbsp
Garlic powder: ½ tsp
Bay seasoning: ½ tsp

**How To Cook:**
Cook crab meat if needed

In a small mixing bowl, mix crab meat with lemon juice and Kewpie mayo and keep aside

In a mixing bowl, beat eggs and add mozzarella cheese to them with garlic powder and bay seasoning

Mix them all well and pour to the greasy mini waffle maker

Cook for at least 4 minutes to get the desired crunch

Remove the chaffle from the heat, add the crab mixture in between and fold

Make as many chaffles as your mixture and waffle maker allow

Serve hot and enjoy!.

## 78. Garlic Lobster Chaffle Roll

Servings: 2
Preparation Time: 5 minutes
Total Time: 10 minutes

**What You Need:**
**For Chaffle:**
Egg: 2
Mozzarella Cheese: 1 cup (shredded)
Bay seasoning: ½ tsp
Garlic powder: ¼ tsp
**For Lobster Mix:**
Langostino Tails: 1 cup
Kewpie Mayo: 2 tbsp
Garlic powder: ½ tsp
Lemon juice: 2 tsp
Parsley: 1 tsp (chopped) for garnishing

**How To Cook:**
Defrost langostino tails
In a small mixing bowl, mix langostino tails with lemon juice, garlic powder, and Kewpie mayo; mix properly and keep aside
In another mixing bowl, beat eggs and add mozzarella cheese to them with garlic powder and bay seasoning
Mix them all well and pour to the greasy mini waffle maker
Cook for at least 4 minutes to get the desired crunch
Remove the chaffle from the heat, add the lobster mixture in between and fold
Make as many chaffles as your mixture and waffle maker allow
Serve hot and enjoy!

## 79. Fried Fish Chaffles

Servings: 2
Preparation Time: 15 minutes
Total Time: 20 minutes

**What You Need:**
**For Chaffle:**
Egg: 2
Mozzarella Cheese: 1 cup (shredded)
Bay seasoning: ½ tsp
Garlic powder: ¼ tsp
**For Fried Fish:**
Fish boneless: 1 cup
Garlic powder: 1 tbsp
Onion powder: 1 tbsp
Salt: ¼ tsp or as per your taste
Black pepper: ¼ tsp or as per your taste
Turmeric: ¼ tsp
Red chili flakes: ½ tbsp
Butter: 2 tbsp

**How To Cook:**
Marinate the fish with all the ingredients of the fried fish except for butter
Melt butter in a medium-size frying pan and add the marinated fish
Fry from both sides for at least 5 minutes and set aside
Preheat a mini waffle maker if needed and grease it
In a mixing bowl, beat eggs and add all the chaffle ingredients
Mix them all well
Pour the mixture to the lower plate of the waffle maker and spread it evenly to cover the plate properly
Close the lid
Cook for at least 4 minutes to get the desired crunch
Remove the chaffle from the heat and keep aside for around one minute
Make as many chaffles as your mixture and waffle maker allow
Serve hot with the prepared fish

## 80. Tuna Melt Chaffle

Servings: 2
Preparation Time: 15 minutes
Total Time: 20 minutes
**What You Need:**
Egg: 1
Mozzarella Cheese: 1/2 cup (shredded)
Tuna: 3 oz without water
Salt: a pinch
**How To Cook:**
Preheat a mini waffle maker if needed and grease it
In a mixing bowl, mix all the ingredients well
Pour the mixture to the lower plate of the waffle maker and spread it evenly to cover the plate properly
Close the lid
Cook for at least 4 minutes to get the desired crunch
Remove the chaffle from the heat and keep aside for around one minute
Make as many chaffles as your mixture and waffle maker allow
Serve hot and enjoy!

# 81. Crispy Crab Chaffle

Servings: 2
Preparation Time: 25 minutes
Total Time: 45 minutes

**What You Need:**
**For Chaffle:**
Egg: 1
Mozzarella Cheese: ½ cup (shredded)
Salt: ¼ tsp or as per your taste
Black pepper: ¼ tsp or as per your taste
Ginger powder: 1 tbsp
**For Crab**
Crab meat: 1 cup
Butter: 2 tbsp
Salt: ¼ tsp or as per your taste
Black pepper: ¼ tsp or as per your taste
Red chili flakes: ½ tsp

**How To Cook:**
In a frying pan, melt butter and fry crab meat for two minutes
Add the spices at the end and set aside
Mix all the chaffle ingredients well together
Pour a thin layer on a preheated waffle iron
Add prepared crab and pour again more mixture over the top
Cook the chaffle for around 5 minutes
Make as many chaffles as your mixture and waffle maker allow
Serve hot with your favorite sauce

# DESERT CHAFFLES

## 82. Keto Icecream Chaffle

Servings: 2
Preparation Time: 15 minutes
Total Time: 30 minutes

**What You Need:**
Egg: 1
Swerve/Monkfruit: 2 tbsp
Baking powder: 1 tbsp
Heavy whipping cream: 1 tbsp
Keto ice cream: as per your choice

**How To Cook:**
Take a small bowl and whisk the egg and add all the ingredients
Beat until the mixture becomes creamy
Pour the mixture to the lower plate of the waffle maker and spread it evenly to cover the plate properly
Close the lid
Cook for at least 4 minutes to get the desired crunch
Remove the chaffle from the heat and keep aside for a few minutes
Make as many chaffles as your mixture and waffle maker allow
Top with your favorite ice cream and enjoy!

## 83. Double Chocolate Chaffle

Servings: 2
Preparation Time: 5 minutes
Total Time: 10 minutes

**What You Need:**
Egg: 2
Coconut flour: 4 tbsp
Cocoa powder: 2 tbsp
Cream cheese: 2 oz
Baking powder: ½ tsp
Chocolate chips: 2 tbsp (unsweetened)
Vanilla extract: 1 tsp
Swerve/Monkfruit: 4 tbsp

**How To Cook:**
Preheat a mini waffle maker if needed and grease it
In a mixing bowl, beat eggs
In a separate mixing bowl, add coconut flour, cocoa powder, Swerve/Monkfruit, and baking powder, when combine pour into eggs with cream cheese and vanilla extracts
Mix them all well to give them uniform consistency and pour the mixture to the lower plate of the waffle maker
On top of the mixture, sprinkle around half tsp of unsweetened chocolate chips and close the lid
Cook for at least 4 minutes to get the desired crunch
Remove the chaffle from the heat and keep aside for around one minute
Make as many chaffles as your mixture and waffle maker allow
Serve with your favorite whipped cream or berries

## 84. Cream Cheese Mini Chaffle

Servings: 2
Preparation Time: 5 minutes
Total Time: 10 minutes

**What You Need:**
Egg: 1
Coconut flour: 2 tbsp
Cream cheese: 1 oz
Baking powder: ¼ tsp
Vanilla extract: ½ tsp
Swerve/Monkfruit: 4 tsp

**How To Cook:**
Preheat a waffle maker if needed and grease it
In a mixing bowl, mix coconut flour, Swerve/Monkfruit, and baking powder
Now add an egg to the mixture with cream cheese and vanilla extract
Mix them all well and pour the mixture to the lower plate of the waffle maker
Close the lid
Cook for at least 4 minutes to get the desired crunch
Remove the chaffle from the heat
Make as many chaffles as your mixture and waffle maker allow
Eat the chaffles with your favorite toppings

## 85. Choco Chip Cannoli Chaffle

Servings: 4
Preparation Time: 10 minutes
Total Time: 20 minutes

**What You Need:**
**For Chaffle:**
Egg yolk: 1
Swerve/Monkfruit: 1 tbsp
Baking powder: 1/8 tbsp
Vanilla extract: 1/8 tsp
Almond flour: 3 tbsp
Chocolate chips: 1 tbsp
**For Cannoli Topping:**
Cream cheese: 4 tbsp
Ricotta: 6 tbsp
Sweetener: 2 tbsp
Vanilla extract: 1/4 tsp
Lemon extract: 5 drops

**How To Cook:**
Preheat a mini waffle maker if needed and grease it
In a mixing bowl, add all the chaffle ingredients and mix well
Pour the mixture to the lower plate of the waffle maker and spread it evenly to cover the plate properly and close the lid
Cook for at least 4 minutes to get the desired crunch
In the meanwhile, prepare cannoli topping by adding all the ingredients in the blender to give the creamy texture
Remove the chaffle from the heat and keep aside to cool them down
Make as many chaffles as your mixture and waffle maker allow
Serve with the cannoli toppings and enjoy

## 86. Cream Cheese Pumpkin Chaffle

Servings: 2
Preparation Time: 5 minutes
Total Time: 10 minutes

**What You Need:**
Egg: 2
Cream cheese: 2 oz
Coconut flour: 2 tsp
Swerve/Monkfruit: 4 tsp
Baking powder: ½ tsp
Vanilla extract: 1 tsp
Canned pumpkin: 2 tbsp
Pumpkin spice: ½ tsp

**How To Cook:**
Take a small mixing bowl and add Swerve/Monkfruit, coconut flour, and baking powder and mix them all well

Now add egg, vanilla extract, pumpkin, and cream cheese, and beat them all together till uniform consistency is achieved

Preheat a mini waffle maker if needed

Pour the mixture to the greasy waffle maker

Cook for at least 4 minutes to get the desired crunch

Remove the chaffle from the heat

Make as many chaffles as your mixture and waffle maker allow

Serve with butter or whipped cream that you like!

## 87. Easy Blueberry Chaffle

Servings: 2
Preparation Time: 5 minutes
Total Time: 10 minutes

**What You Need:**
Egg: 2
Cream cheese: 2 oz
Coconut flour: 2 tbsp
Swerve/Monkfruit: 4 tsp
Baking powder: ½ tsp
Vanilla extract: 1 tsp
Blueberries: ½ cup

**How To Cook:**
Take a small mixing bowl and add Swerve/Monkfruit, baking powder, and coconut flour and mix them all well

Now add eggs, vanilla extract, and cream cheese, and beat them all together till uniform consistency is achieved

Preheat a mini waffle maker if needed and grease it

Pour the mixture to the lower plate of the waffle maker

Add 3-4 fresh blueberries above the mixture and close the lid

Cook for at least 4 minutes to get the desired crunch

Remove the chaffle from the heat

Make as many chaffles as your mixture and waffle maker allow

Serve with butter or whipped cream that you like!

## 88. Apple Pie Chayote Tacos Chaffle

Servings: 2
Preparation Time: 15 minutes
Total Time: 50 minutes

**What You Need:**
**For Chaffle:**
Egg: 2
Cream cheese: ½ cup
Baking powder: 1 tsp
Vanilla extract: ½ tsp
Powdered sweetener: 2 tbsp
**For Apple Pie Chayote Filling:**
Chayote squash: 1
Butter: 1 tbsp
Swerve: ¼ cup
Cinnamon powder: 2 tsp
Lemon: 2 tbsp
Cream of tartar: 1/8 tsp
Nutmeg: 1/8 tsp
Ginger powder: 1/8 tsp

**How To Cook:**
For around 25 minutes, boil the whole chayote; when it cools, peel it and slice

Add all the remaining filling ingredients to it
Bake the chayote for 20 minutes covered with foil
Pour ¼ of the mixtures to the blender to make it a sauce
Add to chayote slices and mix
For the chaffles, preheat a mini waffle maker if needed and grease it
In a mixing bowl, add all the chaffle ingredients and mix well
Pour the mixture to the lower plate of the waffle maker and spread it evenly to cover the plate properly and close the lid
Cook for at least 4 minutes to get the desired crunch
Make as many chaffles as your mixture and waffle maker allow
Fold the chaffles and serve with the chayote sauce in between

## 89. Rice Krispie Treat Copycat Chaffle

Servings: 2
Preparation Time: 15 minutes
Total Time: 25 minutes

**What You Need:**
**For Chaffle:**
Egg: 1
Cream cheese: 4 tbsp
Baking powder: 1 tsp
Vanilla extract: ½ tsp
Powdered sweetener: 2 tbsp
Pork rinds: 4 tbsp (crushed)
**For Marshmallow Frosting:**
Heavy whipping cream: ¼ cup

Xanthan gum: ½ tsp

Powdered sweetener: 1 tbsp
Vanilla extract: ¼ tsp

**How To Cook:**
Preheat a mini waffle maker if needed and grease it
In a mixing bowl, add all the chaffle ingredients
Mix them all well
Pour the mixture to the lower plate of the waffle maker and spread it

evenly to cover the plate properly and close the lid

Cook for at least 4 minutes to get the desired crunch

Remove the chaffle from the heat and keep aside for around one minute

Make as many chaffles as your mixture and waffle maker allow

For the marshmallow frosting, add all the frosting ingredients except xanthan gum and whip to form a thick consistency

Add xanthan gum at the end and fold

Serve frosting with chaffles and enjoy!

## 90. Smores Keto Chaffle

Servings: 2
Preparation Time: 15 minutes
Total Time: 25 minutes

**What You Need:**

Egg: 1
Mozzarella Cheese: ½ cup (shredded)
Baking powder: ¼ tsp
Vanilla extract: ½ tsp
Swerve: 2 tbsp
Pink salt: a pinch
Psyllium husk powder: ½ tbsp
Dark chocolate bar: ¼
Keto Marshmallow crème fluff: 2 tbsp

**How To Cook:**

Create the keto marshmallow crème fluff

Beat the egg that much that it will become creamy and further add Swerve brown and vanilla to it and mix well

Now add cheese to the mixture with Psyllium husk powder, salt, and baking powder and leave chocolate and marshmallow

Mix them all well and allow the batter to set for 3-4 minutes

Preheat a mini waffle maker if needed and grease it

Pour the mixture to the lower plate of the waffle maker and spread it evenly to cover the plate properly

Close the lid

Cook for at least 4 minutes to get the desired crunch

Remove the chaffle from the heat and keep aside for around one minute

Make as many chaffles as your mixture and waffle maker allow

Now serve the chaffle with 2 tbsp marshmallow and chocolate bar

## 91. Maple Iced Soft Cookies Chaffles

Servings: 4
Preparation Time: 20 minutes
Total Time: 45 minutes

**What You Need:**
**For Chaffle Cookie:**
Egg yolk: 1
Cake batter extract: 1/8 tsp
Almond flour: 3 tbsp
Baking powder: 1/8 tsp
Vanilla extract: 1/8 tsp
Sweetener: 1 tbsp
Butter: 1 tbsp
**For Garnishing:**
Nutmeg: for garnishing
Cinnamon powder: 1 tbsp
**For Icing:**
Powdered sweetener: 1 tbsp
Heavy cream: ½ tsp
Maple extract: 1/8 tsp
Water: ½ tsp

**How To Cook:**
Preheat a mini waffle maker if needed and grease it
In a mixing bowl, add all the chaffle ingredients and mix well
Pour the mixture to the lower plate of the waffle maker and spread it evenly to cover the plate properly and cover the lid
Cook for at least 4 minutes to get the desired crunch
Remove the chaffle from the heat and keep aside so it cools down
Make as many chaffles as your mixture and waffle maker allow
For the maple icing, add all the icing ingredient and whisk well
Spread the icing on the chaffle and sprinkle nutmeg and cinnamon on top

## 92. Pumpkin Cookies Chaffle

Servings: 4
Preparation Time: 20 minutes
Total Time: 45 minutes
**What You Need:**
**For Chaffle Cookie:**
Egg yolk: 1
Cake batter extract: 1/8 tsp
Almond flour: 3 tbsp
Baking powder: 1/8 tsp
Vanilla extract: 1/8 tsp
Sweetener: 1 tbsp
Butter: 1 tbsp
**For Icing:**
Powdered sweetener: 1 tbsp
Vanilla extract: ¼ tsp
Water: ½ tsp
**For Sprinkles:**
Granular sweetener: 1 tbsp
Food coloring: 1 drop

**How To Cook:**
Preheat a pumpkin waffle maker if needed and grease it
In a mixing bowl, combine all the chaffle ingredients and mix well
Pour the mixture to the lower plate of the pumpkin waffle maker and spread it evenly to cover the plate properly
Close the lid
Cook for at least 4 minutes to get the desired crunch
Remove the chaffle from the heat and keep aside so it cools down
Make as many chaffles as your mixture and waffle maker allow
For the icing, whisk all the ingredient
Do the same as above for sprinkles
Add these toppings to the chaffles and enjoy

Servings: 4
Preparation Time: 20 minutes
Total Time: 45 minutes

**What You Need:**
**For Chaffle:**
Egg: 2
Mozzarella cheese: ½ cup (grated)
Almond flour: 1 tbsp
Coconut flour: 1 tsp
Baking powder: ½ tsp
**For Apple Fritter Filling:**
Jicama: 2 cups (diced)
Swerve: ¼ cup and 1 tbsp
Cinnamon powder: 1 tsp
Butter: 4 tbsp
Cloves: ½ tbsp (grounded)
Nutmeg: 1/8 tsp
Vanilla: ½ tsp
Apple flavoring: 20 drops
**For Glaze:**
Butter: 1 tbsp
Powdered sweetener: 3 tbsp
Vanilla extract: ¼ tsp
Heavy cream: 2 tsp

**How To Cook:**
Take a small saucepan and melt butter on it on a medium-low heat
Add peeled and cut jicama and allow it to simmer for 20 minutes while stirring in between
It will thicken over time

When jicama becomes soft add the other filling ingredients and remove from heat and keep aside
Preheat a mini waffle maker if needed and grease it
In a mixing bowl, beat eggs and other chaffle ingredients except cheese
Now add the prepared jicama paste to it
Mix them all well
Put around 1 tbsp of grated cheese to the waffle maker's lower plate
Pour the chaffle mixture above the cheese spread it evenly to cover the plate properly
Add 1 tbsp of cheese again on top of the mixture and close the lid
Cook for at least 4 minutes to get the desired crunch
Remove the chaffle from the heat and keep aside for a few minutes
Make as many chaffles as your mixture and waffle maker allow
For the apple fritter icing, melt butter in a small skillet and add heavy cream and the Swerve
Simmer the mixture for 4-5 minutes on a medium-low heat
When it starts to thicken, add vanilla
Pour this hot icing on top of the prepared chaffles; it will become hard when it cools down
)

## 94. Banana Nut Chaffle

Servings: 4
Preparation Time: 10 minutes
Total Time: 20 minutes

**What You Need:**
Egg: 1
Cream cheese: 1 tbsp
Mozzarella cheese: ½ cup
Banana extract: ¼ tbsp
Vanilla extract: ½ tsp
Monkfruit sweetener: 1 tbsp
Caramel sauce: 2 tbsp (sugar-free)
Your favorite nuts: Optional and as much as you like

**How To Cook:**
Preheat a mini waffle maker if needed and grease it

In a mixing bowl, beat eggs and add all the chaffle ingredients except caramel sauce and nuts
Mix them all well
Pour the mixture to the lower plate of the waffle maker and spread it evenly to cover the plate properly
Close the lid
Cook for at least 4 minutes to get the desired crunch
Remove the chaffle from the heat and keep aside for around one minute
Make as many chaffles as your mixture and waffle maker allow
Serve with caramel sauce and your favorite nuts

## 95. Cranberry Swirl Chaffles with Cream Cheese Orange

Servings: 4
Preparation Time: 20 minutes
Total Time: 45 minutes

**What You Need:**
**For Chaffle:**
Egg: 1
Cream cheese: 1 tbsp
Swerve blend: 1 tbsp
Coconut flour: 1 tsp
Vanilla extract: ½ tsp
Baking powder: ¼ tsp
**For Cranberry Sauce:**
Cranberries: ½ cup
Erythritol: 2 tbsp (granulated)
Vanilla extract: ½ tsp
Water: ½ cup
**For Frosting:**
Cream cheese: 2 tbsp
Butter: 1 tbsp
Sweetener: 1 tbsp

Orange zest: 2 tbsp (grated)
Orange extract: 1/8 tsp

**How To Cook:**
Mix cranberries with erythitol, and water in a saucepan and boil on medium-low heat
Simmer the mixture for 15 minutes till the sauce thickens
Remove the mixture from the stove and add vanilla extract
Use a spoon to mash cranberries and heat again for a bit
Preheat a mini waffle maker if needed and grease it
In a mixing bowl, add all the chaffle ingredients and blend
Pour the mixture to the lower plate of the waffle maker and spread it evenly to cover the plate properly

Add cranberry sauce on the top of the mixture in a way that it covers it all and lower the lid

Cook for at least 5 minutes to get the desired crunch

Remove the chaffle from the heat and keep aside for a few minutes to cool them down

Make as many chaffles as your mixture and waffle maker allow

Combine all the ingredients for frosting excluding orange zest and spread over the chaffle

Add orange zest on top at the end before serving

## 96. Oreo Chaffles

Servings: 2
Preparation Time: 10 minutes
Total Time: 15 minutes

**What You Need:**
**For Chaffle:**
Egg: 3
Butter: ½ cup
Chocolate chips: ½ cup (sugar-free)
Truvia: ¼ cup (you can use any other sweetener as well)
Vanilla extract: 1 tsp
**For Cream Cheese Frosting:**
Butter: ½ cup (room temperature)
Cream cheese: ½ cup(room temperature)
Powdered Swerve: ½ cup
Heavy whipping cream: ¼ cup
Vanilla extract: 1 tsp

**How To Cook:**
In a bowl, add butter and chocolate chips and microwave for one minute only

Remove from microwave and stir to melt the chocolate using the butter's heat and set aside

Preheat a mini waffle maker if needed and grease it

In a mixing bowl, beat eggs, and add truvia and vanilla and blend to froth

Now add chocolate and butter in the mixture

Mix them all well and pour the mixture to the lower plate of the waffle maker

Close the lid

Cook for at least 5 minutes to get the desired crunch

Now make the frosting by adding all the frosting ingredients in the food processor and make it smooth

Remove the chaffle from the heat and keep aside for around one minute

In between the two chaffles, put frosting generously to make Oreo Chaffle

Make as many chaffles as your mixture and waffle maker allow

Serve hot and enjoy!

## 97. Banana Cheddar Chaffle

Servings: 4
Preparation Time: 5 minutes
Total Time: 10 minutes

**What You Need:**

Egg: 1
Cream cheese: 1 tbsp
Cheddar cheese: ½ cup
Banana extract: ¼ tbsp
Vanilla extract: ½ tsp
Monkfruit sweetener: 1 tbsp
Caramel sauce: 2 tbsp (sugar-free)

**How To Cook:**

Preheat a mini waffle maker if needed and grease it

In a mixing bowl, beat eggs and add all the chaffle ingredients except caramel sauce

Mix them all well

Pour the mixture to the lower plate of the waffle maker and spread it evenly to cover the plate properly

Close the lid

Cook for at least 4 minutes to get the desired crunch

Remove the chaffle from the heat and keep aside for around one minute

Make as many chaffles as your mixture and waffle maker allow

Serve with caramel sauce

## 98. Chocolate Keto Chaffle

Servings: 2
Preparation Time: 5 minutes
Total Time: 10 minutes

**What You Need:**

Egg: 3
Butter: ½ cup
Chocolate chips: ½ cup (sugar-free)
Truvia: ¼ cup (you can use any other sweetener as well)
Vanilla extract: 1 tsp

**How To Cook:**

In a bowl, add butter and chocolate chips and microwave for one minute only

Remove from microwave and stir to melt the chocolate using the butter's heat and set aside

Preheat a mini waffle maker if needed and grease it

In a mixing bowl, beat eggs, and add truvia and vanilla and blend to froth

Now add chocolate and butter in the mixture

Mix them all well and pour the mixture to the lower plate of the waffle maker

Close the lid

Cook for at least 5 minutes to get the desired crunch

Remove the chaffle from the heat

Make as many chaffles as your mixture and waffle maker allow

Serve with your favorite toppings and enjoy!

## 99. Rutabaga Latkes

Servings: 2
Preparation Time: 5 minutes
Total Time: 10 minutes

**What You Need:**
Egg: 1
Mozzarella cheese: ½ cup
Vanilla Extract: 1/2 tsp
Cinnamon: 1/2 tsp
Monkfruit: 1 tsp (blended)

**How To Cook:**
Preheat a mini waffle maker if needed and grease it

In a mixing bowl, beat eggs and add all the ingredients
Mix them all well and pour the mixture to the lower plate of the waffle maker
Close the lid
Cook for at least 4 minutes to get the desired crunch
Remove the chaffle from the heat and keep aside for around one minute
Make as many chaffles as your mixture and waffle maker allow
Top with your favorite toppings

## 100. Churro Chaffle

Servings: 2
Preparation Time: 5 minutes
Total Time: 10 minutes

**What You Need:**
Egg: 2
Mozzarella Cheese: 1 cup (shredded)
Swerve Brown sweetener: 4 tbsp
Cinnamon powder: 1 tsp

**How To Cook:**
Preheat a mini waffle maker if needed and grease it
In a mixing bowl, beat eggs and add cheese to them

Mix them all well and pour the mixture to the lower plate of the waffle maker
Close the lid
Cook for at least 4 minutes to get the desired crunch
In the meanwhile, mix Swerve Brown sweetener and cinnamon powder in a separate bowl
Remove the chaffle from the heat and cut it into slices when still hot ad add to the cinnamon mixture
Make as many chaffles as your mixture and waffle maker allow
Serve hot and enjoy!

## 101. Crunchy Strawberry Chaffle

Servings: 2
Preparation Time: 5 minutes
Total Time: 10 minutes

**What You Need:**
Egg: 2
Cream cheese: 2 tbsp
Mozzarella Cheese: ½ cup
Baking powder: ½ tsp
Whipping cream: 2 tbsp
Strawberry: 4
Strawberry extract: 2 tsp

**How To Cook:**
Preheat a mini waffle maker if needed and grease it
In a mixing bowl, beat eggs and add mozzarella cheese to them
Now add strawberry extract, cream cheese, and baking powder
Mix them all well and pour the mixture to the lower plate of the waffle maker
Close the lid
Cook for at least 5 minutes to get the desired crunch
Remove the chaffle from the heat and keep aside for around one minute
Make as many chaffles as your mixture and waffle maker allow
Serve with whipped cream and sliced strawberries on top

## 102. Fresh Strawberries Chaffle

Servings: 2
Preparation Time: 5 minutes
Total Time: 10 minutes

**What You Need:**
Egg: 1
Mozzarella Cheese: ½ cup
Almond flour: 1 tbsp
Swerve: 1½ tbsp
Vanilla extract: ¼ tsp
Whipped cream: 2 tbsp
Strawberry: 4

**How to Cook:**
Preheat a mini waffle maker if needed
Chop fresh strawberries and mix with half tablespoon of granulated swerve and keep it aside
In a mixing bowl, beat eggs and add mozzarella cheese, almond flour, granulated swerve, and vanilla extract
Mix them all well and pour the mixture to the lower plate of the waffle maker
Close the lid
Cook for at least 4 minutes to get the desired crunch
Remove the chaffle from the heat and keep aside for around two minute
Make as many chaffles as your mixture and waffle maker allow
Serve with the fresh strawberries mixture you made with the whipped cream on top

## 103. Pecan Pie Cake Chaffle:

Servings: 2
Preparation Time: 15 minutes
Total Time: 25 minutes

**What You Need:**
**For Pecan Pie Chaffle:**
Egg: 1
Cream cheese: 2 tbsp
Maple extract: ½ tbsp
Almond flour: 4 tbsp
Sukrin Gold: 1 tbsp
Baking powder: ½ tbsp
Pecan: 2 tbsp chopped
Heavy whipping cream: 1 tbsp
**For Pecan Pie Filling:**
Butter: 2 tbsp
Sukrin Gold: 1 tbsp
Pecan: 2 tbsp chopped
Heavy whipping cream: 2 tbsp
Maple syrup: 2 tbsp
Egg yolk: 2 large
Salt: a pinch

**How To Cook:**
In a small saucepan, add sweetener, butter, syrups, and heavy whipping cream and use a low flame to heat
Mix all the ingredients well together
Remove from heat and add egg yolks and mix
Now put it on heat again and stir
Add pecan and salt to the mixture and let it simmer
It will thicken then remove from heat and let it rest
For the chaffles, add all the ingredients except pecans and blend
Now add pecan with a spoon
Preheat a mini waffle maker if needed and grease it
Pour the mixture to the lower plate of the waffle maker and spread it evenly to cover the plate properly and close the lid
Cook for at least 4 minutes to get the desired crunch
Remove the chaffle from the heat and keep aside for around one minute
Make as many chaffles as your mixture and waffle maker allow
Add 1/3 the previously prepared pecan pie filling to the chaffle and arrange like a cake)

## 104. Almond Chocolate Chaffle Cake

Servings: 2
Preparation Time: 5 minutes
Total Time: 10 minutes
**What You Need:**
**For Chocolate Chaffle:**
Egg: 1
Cream cheese: 2 tbsp
Powdered sweetener: 1 tbsp
Vanilla extract: ½ tbsp
Instant coffee powder: ¼ tsp
Almond flour: 1 tbsp
Cocoa powder: 1 tbsp (unsweetened)
**For Coconut Filling:**
Melted Coconut Oil: 1 ½ tbsp
Heavy cream: 1 tbsp
Cream cheese: 4 tbsp
Powdered sweetener: 1 tbsp
Vanilla extract: ½ tbsp
Coconut: ¼ cup finely shredded
Whole almonds: 14

**How To Cook:**

Preheat a mini waffle maker if needed and grease it

In a mixing bowl, add all the chaffle ingredients

Mix them all well

Pour the mixture to the lower plate of the waffle maker and spread it evenly to cover the plate properly

Close the lid

Cook for at least 4 minutes to get the desired crunch

Remove the chaffle from the heat and keep aside for around one minute

Make as many chaffles as your mixture and waffle maker allow

Except for almond, add all the filling ingredients in a bowl and mix well

Spread the filling on the chaffle and spread almonds on top with another chaffle at almonds – stack the chaffles and fillings like a cake and enjoy

## 105. German Chocolate Chaffle Cake

Servings: 2
Preparation Time: 5 minutes
Total Time: 10 minutes

**What You Need:**
**For Chocolate Chaffle:**
Egg: 1
Cream cheese: 2 tbsp
Powdered sweetener: 1 tbsp
Vanilla extract: ½ tbsp
Instant coffee powder: ¼ tsp
Almond flour: 1 tbsp
Cocoa powder: 1 tbsp (unsweetened)
**For Filling:**
Egg Yolk: 1
Heavy cream: ¼ cup
Butter: 1 tbsp
Powdered sweetener: 2 tbsp
Caramel: ½ tsp
Coconut flakes: ¼ cup
Coconut flour: 1 tsp
Pecans: ¼ cups chopped

**How To Cook:**
Preheat a mini waffle maker if needed and grease it

In a mixing bowl, beat eggs and add the remaining chaffle ingredients

Mix them all well

Pour the mixture to the lower plate of the waffle maker and spread it evenly to cover the plate properly and close the lid

Cook for at least 4 minutes to get the desired crunch

Remove the chaffle from the heat and let them cool completely

Make as many chaffles as your mixture and waffle maker allow

In a small pan, mix heavy cream, egg yolk, sweetener, and butter at low heat for around 5 minutes

Remove from heat and add the remaining ingredients to make the filling

Stack chaffles on one another and add filling in between to enjoy the cake

## 106. Carrot Cake Chaffle

Servings: 2
Preparation Time: 10 minutes
Total Time: 15 minutes

**What You Need:**
**For Carrot Chaffle Cake:**
Carrot: ½ cup (shredded)
Egg: 1
Heavy whipping cream: 2 tbsp
Butter: 2 tbsp (melted)
Powdered sweetener: 2 tbsp
Walnuts: 1 tbsp (chopped)
Almond flour: ¾ cup
Cinnamon powder: 2 tsp
Baking powder: 1 tsp
Pumpkin sauce: 1 tsp
**For Cream Cheese Frosting:**
Cream cheese: ½ cup
Heavy whipping cream: 2 tbsp
Vanilla extract: 1 tsp
Powdered sweetener: ¼ cup

**How To Cook:**
Mix all the ingredients together one by one until they form a uniform consistency
Preheat a mini waffle maker if needed and grease it
Pour the mixture to the lower plate of the waffle maker
Close the lid
Cook for at least 4 minutes to get the desired crunch
Prepare frosting by combining all the ingredients of the cream cheese frosting using a hand mixer
Remove the chaffle from the heat and keep aside for around a few minutes
Make as many chaffles as your mixture and waffle maker allow
Stack the chaffles with frosting in between in such a way that it gives the look of a cake

## 107. Peanut Butter Keto Chaffle Cake

Servings: 2
Preparation Time: 5 minutes
Total Time: 10 minutes

**What You Need:**
**For Chaffles:**
Egg: 1
Peanut Butter:: 2 tbsp (sugar-free)
Monkfruit: 2 tbsp
Baking powder: ¼ tsp
Peanut butter extract: ¼ tsp
Heavy whipping cream: 1 tsp
**For Peanut Butter Frosting:**
Monkfruit: 2 tsp
Cream cheese: 2 tbsp

Butter: 1 tbsp
Peanut butter: 1 tbsp (sugar-free)
Vanilla: ¼ tsp

**How To Cook:**
Preheat a mini waffle maker if needed and grease it
In a mixing bowl, beat eggs and add all the chaffle ingredients
Mix them all well and pour the mixture to the lower plate of the waffle maker
Close the lid
Cook for at least 4 minutes to get the desired crunch

Remove the chaffle from the heat and keep aside for around a few minutes

Make as many chaffles as your mixture and waffle maker allow

In a separate bowl, add all the frosting ingredients and whisk well to give it a uniform consistency

Assemble chaffles in a way that in between two chaffles you put the frosting and make the cake

## 108. Strawberry Shortcake Chaffle

Servings: 2
Preparation Time: 5 minutes
Total Time: 10 minutes

**What You Need:**
Egg: 1
Heavy Whipping Cream: 1 tbsp
Any non-sugar sweetener: 2 tbsp
Coconut Flour: 1 tsp
Cake batter extract: ½ tsp
Baking powder: ¼ tsp
Strawberry: 4 or as per your taste
**How To Cook:**
Preheat a mini waffle maker if needed and grease it

In a mixing bowl, beat eggs and add non-sugar sweetener, coconut flour, baking powder, and cake batter extract

Mix them all well and pour the mixture to the lower plate of the waffle maker

Close the lid

Cook for at least 4 minutes to get the desired crunch

Remove the chaffle from the heat and keep aside for around two minutes

Make as many chaffles as your mixture and waffle maker allow

Serve with whipped cream and strawberries on top

## 109. Italian Cream Chaffle Cake

Servings: 3
Preparation Time: 8 minutes
Total Time: 12 minutes

**What You Need:**
**For Chaffle:**
Egg: 4
Mozzarella Cheese: ½ cup
Almond flour: 1 tbsp
Coconut flour: 4 tbsp
Monkfruit sweetener: 1 tbsp
Vanilla extract: 1 tsp
Baking powder: 1 ½ tsp

Cinnamon powder: ½ tsp
Butter: 1 tbsp (melted)

Coconut: 1 tsp (shredded)
Walnuts: 1 tsp (chopped)
**For Italian Cream Frosting:**
Cream cheese: 4 tbsp
Butter: 2 tbsp
Vanilla: ½ tsp
Monkfruit sweetener: 2 tbs
**How To Cook:**
Blend eggs, cream cheese, sweetener, vanilla, coconut flour,

melted butter, almond flour, and baking powder

Make the mixture creamy

Preheat a mini waffle maker if needed and grease it

Pour the mixture to the lower plate of the waffle maker

Close the lid

Cook for at least 4 minutes to get the desired crunch

Remove the chaffle from the heat and keep aside to cool it

Make as many chaffles as your mixture and waffle maker allow

Garnish with shredded coconut and chopped walnuts

## 110. Banana Cake Pudding Chaffle

Servings: 2
Preparation Time: 10 minutes
Total Time: 1 hour

**What You Need:**
**For Banana Chaffle:**
Cream cheese: 2 tbsp
Banana extract: 1 tsp
Mozzarella cheese: ¼ cup
Egg: 1
Sweetener: 2 tbsp
Almond flour: 4 tbsp
Baking powder: 1 tsp
**For Banana Pudding:**
Egg yolk: 1 large
Powdered sweetener: 3 tbsp
Xanthan gum: ½ tsp
Heavy whipping cream: 1/2 cup
Banana extract: ½ tsp
Salt: a pinch

**How To Cook:**
In a pan, add powdered sweetener, heavy cream, and egg yolk and whisk continuously so the mixture thickens

Simmer for a minute only

Add xanthan gum to the mixture and whisk again

Remove the pan from heat and add banana extract and salt and mix them all well

Shift the mixture to a glass dish and refrigerate the pudding

Preheat a mini waffle maker if needed and grease it

In a mixing bowl, add all the chaffle ingredients

Mix them all well and pour the mixture to the lower plate of the waffle maker

Close the lid

Cook for at least 5 minutes to get the desired crunch

Remove the chaffle from the heat and keep aside for around a few minutes

Stack chaffles and pudding one by one to form a cake

# 111. Cream Coconut Chaffle Cake

Servings: 2
Preparation Time: 20 minutes
Total Time: 1 hour 20 minutes
(depends on your refrigerator)

**What You Need:**
**For Chaffles:**
Egg: 2
Powdered sweetener: 2 tbsp
Cream cheese: 2 tbsp
Vanilla extract: 1/2 tsp
Butter: 1 tbsp (melted)
Coconut: 2 tbsp (shredded)
Coconut extract: ½ tsp
**For Filling:**
Coconut: ¼ cup (shredded)
Butter: 2 tsp
Monkfruit sweetener: 2 tbsp
Xanthan gum: ¼ tsp
Salt: a pinch
Egg yolks: 2
Almond: 1/3 cup unsweetened
Coconut milk: 1/3 cup
**For Garnishing:**
Whipped Cream: as per your taste
Coconut: 1 tbsp (shredded)

**How To Cook:**
Preheat a mini waffle maker if needed and grease it
In a mixing bowl, add all the chaffle ingredients

Mix them all well and pour the mixture to the lower plate of the waffle maker
Close the lid
Cook for at least 4 minutes to get the desired crunch
Remove the chaffle from the heat and keep aside for around a few minutes
Make as many chaffles as your mixture and waffle maker allow
For the filling, in a small pan, cook almond milk and coconut together on medium heat in such way that it only steams but doesn't boil
In another bowl, lightly whish egg yolks and add milk to it continuously
Heat the mixture so it thickens, again it must not boil
Add sweetener and whisk while adding Xanthan Gum bit by bit
Remove from heat and mix all the other ingredients
Mix well and refrigerate; the mixture will further thicken when cool
Assemble the prepared chaffles and cream on top of one another to make the cake-like shape
Garnish with coconuts and whipped cream at the end
)

## 112. Lemon Chaffle Cake

Servings: 2
Preparation Time: 20 minutes
Total Time: 40 minutes (depends on chaffle's cooling)

**What You Need:**
**For Chaffles:**
Egg: 2
Powdered sweetener: 1 tbsp
Cream cheese: 4 tbsp
Butter: 2 tbsp (melted)
Coconut flour: 2 tsp
Baking powder: 1 tsp
Lemon extract: ½ tsp
Cake batter extract: 20 drops
**For Frosting:**
Heavy whipping cream: ½ cup
Monkfruit sweetener: 1 tbsp
Lemon extract: ¼ tsp

**How To Cook:**
Preheat a mini waffle maker if needed and grease it
In a blender, add all the chaffle ingredients and blend
Pour the mixture to the lower plate of the waffle maker and spread it evenly to cover the plate properly
Close the lid
Cook for at least 4 minutes to get the desired crunch
Remove the chaffle from the heat and keep aside
Make as many chaffles as your mixture and waffle maker allow
Prepare the frosting by whisking all the frosting ingredients till it thickens and attains uniform consistency
When all the chaffles cool down, arrange in the form of cake by adding frosting in between

## 113. Keto Birthday Chaffle Cake

Servings: 2
Preparation Time: 20 minutes
Total Time: 40 minutes

**What You Need:**
**For Chaffle:**
Egg: 2
Powdered sweetener: 2 tbsp
Cream cheese: 2 tbsp
Butter: 2 tbsp (melted)
Coconut flour: 2 tsp
Almond flour: ¼ cup
Baking powder: ½ tsp
Vanilla extract: ½ tsp
Xanthan powder ¼ tsp
**For Frosting:**
Heavy whipping cream: 1/2 cup

Swerve: 2 tbsp

Vanilla extract: ½ tsp

**How To Cook:**
Preheat a mini waffle maker if needed
In a medium-size blender, add all the cake ingredients and blend till it forms a creamy texture
Let the batter sit for a minute or two; appearance is watery but it produces crunchy chaffles
Pour the batter to the lower plate of the waffle maker and spread it evenly to cover the plate properly
Close the lid

72

Cook for at least 4 minutes to get the desired crunch

Remove the chaffle from the heat and keep aside to cool totally

For the frosting, add all the ingredients in a bowl and use a hand mixer until the cream thickens

Make as many chaffles as your mixture and waffle maker allow

Frost the chaffles in a way you like

Serve cool and enjoy!

## 114. Tiramasu Chaffle Cake

Servings: 4
Preparation Time: 20 minutes
Total Time: 40 minutes

**What You Need:**
Egg: 2
Monkfruit sweetener: 2 tbsp
Cream cheese: 2 tbsp
Butter: 2 tbsp (melted)
Coconut flour: 2 tbsp
Baking powder: 1 tsp
Vanilla extract: ½ tsp
Instant coffee dry mix: 2 ½ tsp
Hazelnut extract: ½ tsp
Almond flour: ¼ cup
Organic cacao powder: 1 ½ tbsp
Himalayan pink fine salt: 1/8 tsp
Mascarpone Cheese: ½ cup
Powdered sweetener: ¼ cup

**How To Cook:**
In a microwave, melt butter for a minute and then add instant coffee, stir it continuously

In a bowl, beat eggs, cream cheese and the butter-coffee mixture

In a separate bowl, add sweetener, vanilla extract, and mascarpone cheese

In the egg mixture, add all the dry ingredients into it and mix well

Preheat a mini waffle maker if needed and grease it

Pour the egg mixture to the lower plate of the waffle maker and spread it evenly to cover the plate properly and close the lid

Cook for at least 4 minutes to get the desired crunch

Remove the chaffle from the heat and keep aside to cool down

Make as many chaffles as your mixture and waffle maker allow

If you want to have two layers cake then split the cream

You can also separate cacao powder ½ tbsp and instant coffee ½ tsp and blend

Layer the cake in a way that spread cream and coffee mixture on one chaffle and add another chaffle on top

Serve cool and enjoy!

# SAUSAGE CHAFFLES
## 115. Sausage Ball Keto Chaffle

Servings: 4
Preparation Time: 5 minutes
Total Time: 10 minutes

**What You Need:**
Egg: 1
Cheddar cheese: 1 cup (shredded)
Parmesan cheese: ¼ cup (grated)
Italian sausage: 1 pound
Baking powder: 2 tsp
Almond flour: 1 tbsp

**How To Cook:**
Preheat a mini waffle maker if needed and grease it

I

n a mixing bowl, beat eggs and add all the remaining ingredients one by one
Mix them all well and pour the mixture to the lower plate of the waffle maker
Close the lid
Cook for at least 4 minutes to get the desired crunch
Remove the chaffle from the heat
Make as many chaffles as your mixture and waffle maker allow
Serve hot and enjoy!

## 116. Corndog Chaffle

Servings: 2
Preparation Time: 5 minutes
Total Time: 10 minutes

**What You Need:**
Egg: 1
Butter: 1 ½ tsp
Sweetener: 2 tsp
Cornbread flavoring: 15-20 drops
Baking powder: ¼ tsp
Egg yolk: 1 egg
Almond flour: 3 tbsp
Mexican blend cheese: 2 tbsp
Pickled Jalapenos: 1 tbsp
Hot dog: 2
Mustard: For flavoring

**How To Cook:**
Preheat a mini waffle maker if needed and grease it

In a mixing bowl, add all the ingredients except hot dogs and mustard
Mix them all well
Pour the mixture to the lower plate of the waffle maker and spread it evenly to cover the plate properly and close the lid
Cook for at least 4 minutes to get the desired crunch
Remove the chaffle from the heat and keep aside for around one minute
Make as many chaffles as your mixture and waffle maker allow
Fold by placing a hot dog in between and spread mustard on top
Serve hot and enjoy!.

# VEGETABLE CHAFFLES
## 117. Okra Fritter Chaffle

Servings: 2
Preparation Time: 10 minutes
Total Time: 20 minutes
**What You Need:**
Egg: 1
Mozzarella cheese: ¼ cup
Onion powder: ½ tbsp
Heavy cream: 2 tbsp
Mayo: 1 tbsp
Garlic: 2 cloves (finely chopped)
Almond flour: ¼ cup
Okra: 1 cup
Salt: ¼ tsp or as per your taste
Black pepper: ¼ tsp or as per your taste

**How To Cook:**
Combine egg, mayo, and heavy cream and whisk

When mixed, add almond flour and make a uniform batter
Leave it for 5-10 minutes
Now add okra and rest of the ingredients and mix well
Preheat a mini waffle maker if needed and grease it
Pour the mixture to the lower plate of the waffle maker and spread it evenly to cover the plate properly
Close the lid
Cook for at least 4 minutes to get the desired crunch
Remove the chaffle from the heat
Make as many chaffles as your mixture and waffle maker allow
Serve hot and enjoy!

## 118. Spinach Zucchini Chaffle

Servings: 2
Preparation Time: 10 minutes
Total Time: 15 minutes

**What You Need:**
Zucchini: 1 (small)
Egg: 1
Shredded mozzarella: half cup
Parmesan: 1 tbsp
Pepper: As per your taste
Basil: 1 tsp
Spinach: ½ cup

**How To Cook:**
Preheat your waffle iron

Grate zucchini finely
Boil spinach for five minutes and strain water
Add all the ingredients to zucchini in a bowl and mix well
Now add the spinach
Grease your waffle iron lightly
Pour the mixture into a full-size waffle maker and spread evenly
Cook till it turns crispy
Make as many chaffles as your mixture and waffle maker allow
Serve crispy and with your favorite keto sauce

## 119. Okra Cauli Chaffle

Servings: 2
Preparation Time: 10 minutes
Total Time: 15 minutes

**What You Need:**
Cauliflower: 1/2 cup
Okra: ½ cup
Egg: 2
Mozzarella Cheese: 1 cup (shredded)
Butter: 1 tbsp
Almond flour: 2 tbsp
Turmeric: ¼ tsp
Baking powder: ¼ tsp
Onion powder: a pinch
Garlic powder: a pinch
Salt: a pinch

**How To Cook:**
In a deep saucepan, boil okra and cauliflower for five minutes or till it tenders, strain and set aside
Mix all the remaining ingredients well together
Pour a thin layer on a preheated waffle iron
Remove any excess water from the vegetables and add a layer on the mixture
Again add more mixture over the top
Cook the chaffle for around 5 minutes
Serve hot with your favorite keto sauce.

## 120. Crispy Cauli Chaffle

Servings: 2
Preparation Time: 5 minutes
Total Time: 10 minutes
**What You Need:**
Cauliflower rice: 1 cup
Egg: 1
Parmesan cheese: ½ cup (shredded)
Mozzarella Cheese: ½ cup (shredded)
Salt: ¼ tsp or as per your taste
Black pepper: ¼ tsp or as per your taste
Italian seasoning: ½ tsp
Garlic powder: ½ tsp
**How To Cook:**
Preheat a mini waffle maker if needed and grease it
Add all the ingredients, except for parmesan cheese, into a blender
Mix them all well
Spread 1/8 cup of shredded parmesan cheese to the lower plate of the waffle maker
Pour the cauliflower mixture above the cheese
Again sprinkle 1/8 cup of shredded parmesan cheese on top of the mixture
Close the lid
Cook for at least 5 minutes to get the desired crunch
Remove the chaffle from the heat
Serve hot and enjoy!.

## 121.Seafood Jambalaya

Servings: 2
Preparation Time: 5 minutes
Total Time: 10 minutes

**What You Need:**
Egg: 2
Cheddar cheese: 1 cup
Onion: ½ medium minced
Jicama root: 1 large
Garlic: 2 cloves
Salt: ¼ tsp or as per your taste
Black pepper: ¼ tsp or as per your taste

**How To Cook:**
With peeler or knife, peel jicama and blend it in a food processor
Put this in a large colander with a pinch of salt and let it drain
Make it dry as much as possible

Microwave it for around 7 minutes
Now add the remaining ingredients to the blended jicama and mix well
Preheat a mini waffle maker if needed and grease it
Pour the mixture to the lower plate of the waffle maker and spread it evenly to cover the plate properly
Close the lid
Cook for at least 4 minutes to get the desired crunch
Remove the chaffle from the heat
Make as many chaffles as your mixture and waffle maker allow
Serve hot and enjoy!

.

## 122. Spinach Garlic Butter Chaffle

Servings: 2
Preparation Time: 15 minutes
Total Time: 20 minutes
**What You Need:**
**For the Chaffle:**
Egg: 2
Mozzarella Cheese: 1 cup (shredded)
Garlic powder: ½ tsp
Italian seasoning: 1 tsp
Cream cheese: 1 tsp
Spinach: ½ cup
**For the Garlic Butter Topping:**
Garlic powder: ½ tsp
Italian seasoning: 1/2 tsp
Butter: 1 tbsp

**How To Cook:**
In a small saucepan, add ¼ cup water with spinach and simmer for 5 minutes

Drain the excess water from spinach and set aside
Preheat a mini waffle maker if needed and grease it
In a mixing bowl, add all the ingredients of the chaffle along with the prepared spinach and mix well
Pour the mixture to the lower plate of the waffle maker and spread it evenly to cover the plate properly and close the lid
Cook for at least 4 minutes to get the desired crunch
In the meanwhile, melt butter and add the garlic butter ingredients
Remove the chaffle from the heat and apply the garlic butter immediately
Make as many chaffles as your mixture and waffle maker allow)

## 123. All Green Chaffle

Servings: 4
Preparation Time: 10 minutes
Total Time: 15 minutes

**What You Need:**
**For Chaffle:**
Cabbage: 1/2 cup
Broccoli: ½ cup
Zucchini: ½ cup
Egg: 2
Mozzarella Cheese: 1 cup (shredded)
Butter: 1 tbsp
Almond flour: 2 tbsp
Baking powder: ¼ tsp
Onion powder: a pinch
Garlic powder: a pinch
Salt: a pinch
**For Filling:**
Cucumber: ½ cup diced
Lettuce leave: 4

**How To Cook:**
In a deep saucepan, boil cabbage, broccoli, and zucchini for five minutes or till it tenders, strain and blend
Mix all the remaining ingredients well together
Pour a thin layer on a preheated waffle iron
Add a layer of the blended vegetables on the mixture
Again add more mixture over the top
Cook the chaffle for around 5 minutes
Remove from heat, fold and add lettuce and cucumber
Serve with your favorite sauce

## 124. Broccoli Cauli Cabbage Chaffle

Servings: 4
Preparation Time: 10 minutes
Total Time: 15 minutes

**What You Need:**
Cauliflower: 1/2 cup
Cabbage: 1/2 cup
Broccoli: ½ cup
Egg: 2
Mozzarella Cheese: 1 cup (shredded)
Butter: 1 tbsp
Almond flour: 2 tbsp
Turmeric: ¼ tsp
Baking powder: ¼ tsp
Onion powder: a pinch
Garlic powder: a pinch
Salt: a pinch

**How To Cook:**
In a deep saucepan, boil cabbage, broccoli, and cauliflower for five minutes or till it tenders, strain and set aside
Mix all the remaining ingredients well together
Pour a thin layer on a preheated waffle iron
Remove any excess water from the vegetables and add a layer on the mixture
Again add more mixture over the top
Cook the chaffle for around 5 minutes
Serve hot with your favorite keto sauce

## 125. Peppermint Mocha Chaffle

Servings: 2
Preparation Time: 10 minutes
Total Time: 20 minutes

**What You Need:**
**For Chaffle:**
Egg: 1
Powdered sweetener: 2 tbsp
Cream cheese: 2 tbsp
Butter: 2 tbsp (melted)
Coconut flour: 2 tsp
Almond flour: 1 tsp
Baking powder: 1/4 tsp
Vanilla extract: ¼ tsp
Cocoa powder: 1 tbsp (unsweetened)
Salt: a pinch
**For Filling:**
Heavy cream: ½ cup
Powdered sweetener: 2 tbsp
Butter: 2 tbsp
Vanilla extract: ¼ tsp
Peppermint extract: 1/8 tsp
Starlight mints: for garnishing

**How To Cook:**
Preheat a mini waffle maker if needed and grease it
In a mixing bowl, add all the chaffle ingredients
Mix them all well
Pour the mixture to the lower plate of the waffle maker and spread it evenly to cover the plate properly and close the lid
Cook for at least 4 minutes to get the desired crunch
Remove the chaffle from the heat and keep aside for around one minute
Make as many chaffles as your mixture and waffle maker allow
For the filling, add all the filling ingredients and beat at high speed using the hand blender
On each chaffle spread the filling and top with starlight mint

## 126. Easy Broccoli Chaffle

Servings: 2
Preparation Time: 5 minutes
Total Time: 10 minutes
**What You Need:**
Broccoli: 1 cup
Egg: 2
Mozzarella Cheese: 1 cup (shredded)
Butter: 1 tbsp
Almond flour: 2 tbsp
Turmeric: ¼ tsp
Baking powder: ¼ tsp
Onion powder: a pinch
Garlic powder: a pinch
Salt: a pinch

**How To Cook:**
In a deep saucepan, boil broccoli for five minutes or till it tenders, strain and set aside
Mix all the remaining ingredients well together
Pour a thin layer on a preheated waffle iron
Remove any excess water from broccoli and add 1 tbsp of broccoli to the mixture
Again add more mixture over the top
Cook the chaffle for around 5 minutes
Serve hot with your favorite keto sauce

## 127. Spinach and Cabbage Chaffle

Servings: 2
Preparation Time: 10 minutes
Total Time: 15 minutes

**What You Need:**
**For the Chaffle:**
Egg: 2
Mozzarella Cheese: 1 cup (shredded)
Butter: 1 tbsp
Almond flour: 2 tbsp
Turmeric: ¼ tsp
Baking powder: ¼ tsp
Onion powder: a pinch
Garlic powder: a pinch
Salt: a pinch
Black pepper: ¼ tsp or as per your taste
Spinach: ½ cup
Cabbage: ½ cup

**How To Cook:**
Boil the spinach and cabbage in water for around 10 minutes and drain the remaining water
In a mixing bowl, add all the above-mentioned ingredients except
Mix well and add the boiled spinach
Pour the mixture to the lower plate of the waffle maker and spread it evenly to cover the plate properly
Cook for at least 4 minutes to get the desired crunch
Remove the chaffle from the heat
Make as many chaffles as your mixture and waffle maker allow
Serve hot and enjoy!

## 128. Garlic Broccoli Chaffle

Servings: 2
Preparation Time: 15 minutes
Total Time: 20 minutes

**What You Need:**
**For the Chaffle:**
Egg: 2
Mozzarella Cheese: 1 cup (shredded)
Garlic powder: ½ tsp
Italian seasoning: 1 tsp
Cream cheese: 1 tsp
**For the Garlic Butter Topping:**
Garlic powder: ½ tsp
Italian seasoning: 1/2 tsp
Butter: 1 tbsp
**For Broccoli:**
Broccoli: ½ cup

Salt: ¼ tsp or as per your taste
Black pepper: ¼ tsp or as per your taste

**How To Cook:**
In a small saucepan, add broccoli and water and boil for 10 minutes
When it tenders, remove from water and blend with hand mixer and add salt and pepper
Preheat a mini waffle maker if needed and grease it
In a mixing bowl, add all the ingredients of the chaffle and mix well
Pour the thin layer of the mixture to the lower plate of the waffle maker

and spread it evenly to cover the plate properly

Add 1/2 tablespoon of the broccoli paste over the mixture

Add thin layer of chaffle mixture again on the broccoli paste

Cook for at least 4 minutes to get the desired crunch

In the meanwhile, melt butter and add the garlic butter ingredients

Remove the chaffle from the heat and apply the garlic butter immediately and serve hot

## 129. Jalapeno Zucchini Chaffle

Servings: 2
Preparation Time: 10 minutes
Total Time: 15 minutes

**What You Need:**

Zucchini: 1 small
Onion powder: 1/8 tsp
Garlic powder: 1/8 tsp
Egg: 1
Cheddar cheese: 1/4 cup
Jalapeno: 1 diced
Cream cheese: 1 tbsp
Parmesan cheese: 1/8 tbsp

**How To Cook:**

Preheat a mini waffle maker if needed and grease it

In a mixing bowl, beat eggs and add all the ingredients

Mix them all well

Pour the mixture to the lower plate of the waffle maker and spread it evenly to cover the plate properly

Close the lid

Cook for at least 4 minutes to get the desired crunch

Remove the chaffle from the heat and keep aside for around one minute

Make as many chaffles as your mixture and waffle maker allow

Serve hot and enjoy!

## 130. Crispy Broccoli and Artichok Chaffle

Servings: 2
Preparation Time: 10 minutes
Total Time: 20 minutes

**What You Need:**
Artichokes: 1/2 cup chopped
Broccoli: ½ cup chopped and boiled
Egg: 1
Mozzarella Cheese: 1/2 cup (shredded)
Cream cheese: 1 ounce
Salt: as per your taste
Pepper: as per your taste
Garlic powder: ¼ tsp

**How To Cook:**
Preheat a mini waffle maker if needed and grease it
In a mixing bowl, add all the ingredients
Mix them all well
Pour the mixture to the lower plate of the waffle maker and spread it evenly to cover the plate properly
Close the lid
Cook for at least 4 minutes to get the desired crunch
Remove the chaffle from the heat and keep aside for around one minute
Make as many chaffles as your mixture and waffle maker allow
Serve hot with your favorite keto sauce

## 131. Olive and Spinach Chaffles

Servings: 2
Preparation Time: 10 minutes
Total Time: 15 minutes

**What You Need:**
**For the Chaffle:**
Egg: 2
Mozzarella Cheese: 1 cup (shredded)
Butter: 1 tbsp
Almond flour: 2 tbsp
Turmeric: ¼ tsp
Baking powder: ¼ tsp
Onion powder: a pinch
Garlic powder: a pinch
Salt: a pinch
Black pepper: ¼ tsp or as per your taste
Spinach: ½ cup
Olives: 5-10

**How To Cook:**
Boil the spinach in water for around 10 minutes and drain the remaining water
In a mixing bowl, add all the above-mentioned ingredients except for olives
Mix well and add the boiled spinach
Pour the mixture to the lower plate of the waffle maker and spread it evenly to cover the plate properly
Sprinkle the sliced olives as per choice over the mixture and close the lid
Cook for at least 4 minutes to get the desired crunch
Remove the chaffle from the heat
Make as many chaffles as your mixture and waffle maker allow
Serve hot and enjoy!.

## 132 Simple Cabbage Chaffles

Servings: 2
Preparation Time: 10 minutes
Total Time: 15 minutes

**What You Need:**
Egg: 2
Mozzarella Cheese: 1 cup (shredded)
Butter: 2 tbsp
Almond flour: 2 tbsp
Turmeric: ¼ tsp
Baking powder: ¼ tsp
Onion powder: a pinch
Garlic powder: a pinch
Salt: as per your taste
Cabbage: 1 cup shredded

**How To Cook:**
Take a frying pan and melt 1 tbsp of butter
Add the shredded cabbage and sauté for 4 minutes and set aside
In a mixing bowl, add all the ingredients and mix well
Pour a thin layer on a preheated waffle iron
Add cabbage on top of the mixture
Again add more mixture over the top
Cook the chaffle for around 5 minutes
Serve hot with your favorite keto sauce
.

## 133. Cabbage and Artichoke Chaffle

Servings: 2
Preparation Time: 10 minutes
Total Time: 20 minutes

**What You Need:**
Artichokes: 1/2 cup chopped
Cabbage: ½ cup
Black pepper: ½ tbsp
Egg: 1
Mozzarella Cheese: 1/2 cup (shredded)
Cream cheese: 1 ounce
Salt: as per your taste
Garlic powder: ¼ tsp
Turmeric: ¼ tsp
Baking powder: ¼ tsp

**How To Cook:**
Take a frying pan and melt 1 tbsp of butter
Add the shredded cabbage and sauté for 4 minutes and set aside
In a mixing bowl, add all the ingredients and mix well
Pour a thin layer on a preheated waffle iron
Add cabbage on top of the mixture
Again add more mixture over the top
Cook the chaffle for around 5 minutes
Serve hot with your favorite keto sauce

## 134. Zucchini BBQ Chaffle

Servings: 2
Preparation Time: 10 minutes
Total Time: 20 minutes

**What You Need:**
Zucchini: 1/2 cup
BBQ sauce: 1 tbsp (sugar-free)
Almond flour: 2 tbsp
Egg: 1
Cheddar cheese: ½ cup

**How To Cook:**
Finely grate zucchini
Preheat your waffle iron

In mixing bowl, add all the chaffle ingredients including zucchini and mix well
Grease your waffle iron lightly
Pour the mixture to the bottom plate evenly; also spread it out to get better results and close the upper plate and heat
Cook for 6 minutes or until the chaffle is done
Make as many chaffles as your mixture and waffle maker allow

## 135. Eggplant BBQ Chaffle

Servings: 2
Preparation Time: 10 minutes
Total Time: 20 minutes

**What You Need:**
Egg plant: 1/2 cup
BBQ sauce: 1 tbsp (sugar-free)
Almond flour: 2 tbsp
Egg: 1
Cheddar cheese: ½ cup

**How To Cook:**
Boil egg plant in water, and strain
Preheat your waffle iron

In mixing bowl, add all the chaffle ingredients including zucchini and mix well
Grease your waffle iron lightly
Pour the mixture to the bottom plate evenly; also spread it out to get better results and close the upper plate and heat
Cook for 6 minutes or until the chaffle is done
Make as many chaffles as your mixture and waffle maker allow)

## 136. Zucchini Olives Chaffles

Servings: 2
Preparation Time: 10 minutes
Total Time: 15 minutes
**What You Need:**
Egg: 2
Mozzarella Cheese: 1 cup (shredded)
Butter: 1 tbsp
Almond flour: 2 tbsp
Turmeric: ¼ tsp
Baking powder: ¼ tsp
Onion powder: a pinch
Garlic powder: a pinch
Salt: a pinch
Black pepper: ¼ tsp or as per your taste
Spinach: ½ cup
Olives: 5-10
**How To Cook:**
Boil the spinach in water for around 10 minutes and drain the remaining water

In a mixing bowl, add all the above-mentioned ingredients except for olives
Mix well and add the boils spinach
Pour the mixture to the lower plate of the waffle maker and spread it evenly to cover the plate properly
Sprinkle the sliced olives as per choice over the mixture and close the lid
Cook for at least 4 minutes to get the desired crunch
Remove the chaffle from the heat
Make as many chaffles as your mixture and waffle maker allow
Serve hot and enjoy!

## 137. Cauliflower Mozzarella Chaffle

Servings: 2
Preparation Time: 15 minutes
Total Time: 25 minutes

**What You Need:**
Cauliflower: 1 cup
Egg: 2
Mozzarella cheese: 1 cup and 4 tbsp
Tomato sauce: 6 tbsp
Basil: ½ tsp
Garlic: ½ tbsp
Butter: 1 tsp

**How To Cook:**
In a pan, add butter and include small pieces of cauliflower to it
Stir for two minutes and then add garlic and basil

Set aside the cooked cauliflower
Preheat the mini waffle maker if needed
Mix cooked cauliflower, eggs, and 1 cup mozzarella cheese properly
Spread it to the mini waffle maker thoroughly
Cook for 4 minutes or till it turns crispy and then remove it from the waffle maker
Make as many mini chaffles as you can
Now in a baking tray, line these mini chaffles and top with the tomato sauce and grated mozzarella cheese
Put the tray in the oven at 400 degrees until the cheese melts
Serve hot

## 138. Plain Artichok Chaffle

Servings: 2
Preparation Time: 10 minutes
Total Time: 20 minutes

**What You Need:**

Artichokes: 1 cup chopped
Egg: 1
Mozzarella Cheese: 1/2 cup (shredded)
Cream cheese: 1 ounce
Salt: as per your taste
Garlic powder: ¼ tsp

**How To Cook:**

Preheat a mini waffle maker if needed and grease it

In a mixing bowl, add all the ingredients
Mix them all well
Pour the mixture to the lower plate of the waffle maker and spread it evenly to cover the plate properly
Close the lid
Cook for at least 4 minutes to get the desired crunch
Remove the chaffle from the heat and keep aside for around one minute
Make as many chaffles as your mixture and waffle maker allow
Serve hot with your favorite keto sauce

## 139. Eggplant and Artichok Chaffle

Servings: 2
Preparation Time: 10 minutes
Total Time: 20 minutes

**What You Need:**

Artichokes: 1/2 cup chopped
Eggplant: ½ cup chopped and boiled
Egg: 1
Mozzarella Cheese: 1/2 cup (shredded)
Cream cheese: 1 ounce
Salt: as per your taste
Pepper: as per your taste
Garlic powder: ¼ tsp

**How To Cook:**

Preheat a mini waffle maker if needed and grease it

In a mixing bowl, add all the ingredients
Mix them all well
Pour the mixture to the lower plate of the waffle maker and spread it evenly to cover the plate properly
Close the lid
Cook for at least 4 minutes to get the desired crunch
Remove the chaffle from the heat and keep aside for around one minute
Make as many chaffles as your mixture and waffle maker allow
Serve hot with your favorite keto sauce

## 140. Sliced Eggplant Chaffles

Servings: 2
Preparation Time: 15 minutes
Total Time: 20 minutes

**What You Need:**
**For Chaffles:**
Eggs: 2
Cheddar cheese: ½ cup
Parmesan cheese: 2 tbsp
Italian season: ¼ tsp
**For Egg Plant:**
Eggplant: 1 big
Salt: 1 pinch
Black pepper: 1 pinch

**How To Cook:**
Cut the eggplant in slices and boil in water and strain
Add a pinch of salt and pepper

Add all the chaffle ingredients in a bowl and mix well to make a mixture
Preheat a mini waffle maker if needed and grease it
Pour the mixture to the lower plate of the waffle maker and spread it evenly to cover the plate properly
Add the eggplant over two slices on the mixture and cover the lid
Cook for at least 4 minutes to get the desired crunch
Remove the chaffle from the heat and keep aside for around one minute
Make as many chaffles as your mixture and waffle maker allow
Serve hot with your favorite sauce

## 141. Artichoke and Spinach Chaffle

Servings: 2
Preparation Time: 10 minutes
Total Time: 20 minutes

**What You Need:**
Spinach: 1/2 cup cooked and chopped
Artichokes: 1/2 cup chopped
Egg: 1
Mozzarella Cheese: 1/2 cup (shredded)
Cream cheese: 1 ounce
Garlic powder: ¼ tsp

**How To Cook:**
Preheat a mini waffle maker if needed and grease it

In a mixing bowl, add all the ingredients
Mix them all well
Pour the mixture to the lower plate of the waffle maker and spread it evenly to cover the plate properly
Close the lid
Cook for at least 4 minutes to get the desired crunch
Remove the chaffle from the heat and keep aside for around one minute
Make as many chaffles as your mixture and waffle maker allow
Serve hot and enjoy!

## 142. Jalapeno Cauli Chaffle

Servings: 2
Preparation Time: 10 minutes
Total Time: 15 minutes

**What You Need:**
Cauliflower rice: 1 cup
Onion powder: 1/4 tsp
Garlic powder: 1/4 tsp
Egg: 1
Cheddar cheese: 1/4 cup
Jalapeno: 1 diced
Cream cheese: 1 tbsp
Parmesan cheese: 1/8 tbsps
Salt: as per your taste

**How To Cook:**
Preheat a mini waffle maker if needed and grease it

In a mixing bowl, beat egg and add all the ingredients
Mix them all well
Pour the mixture to the lower plate of the waffle maker and spread it evenly to cover the plate properly
Close the lid
Cook for at least 4 minutes to get the desired crunch
Remove the chaffle from the heat and keep aside for around one minute
Make as many chaffles as your mixture and waffle maker allow
Serve hot and enjoy!
)

## 143. Zucchini Mozzarella Chaffle

Servings: 2
Preparation Time: 5 minutes
Total Time: 10 minutes

**What You Need:**
Egg: 2
Zucchini: 1 small
Mozzarella cheese: 1 cup and 4 tbsp
Tomato sauce: 6 tbsp
Basil: ½ tsp
Garlic: ½ tbsp
Butter: 1 tsp

**How To Cook:**
Grate zucchini finely
Add garlic and basil to it with eggs, butter, and mozzarella cheese

Preheat the mini waffle maker if needed
Spread the mixture to the mini waffle maker thoroughly
Cook for 4 minutes or till it turns crispy and then remove it from the waffle maker
Make as many mini chaffles as you can
Now in a baking tray, line these mini chaffles and top with the tomato sauce and grated mozzarella cheese
Put the tray in the oven at 400 degrees until the cheese melts
Serve hot with your favorite sauce

## 144. Egg Plant Mozzarella Chaffle

Servings: 2
Preparation Time: 15 minutes
Total Time: 25 minutes

**What You Need:**

Eggplant: 1 cup
Egg: 2
Mozzarella cheese: 1 cup and 4 tbsp
Tomato sauce: 6 tbsp
Basil: ½ tsp
Garlic: ½ tbsp
Butter: 1 tsp

**How To Cook:**

In a pan, add butter and include grated eggplant
Stir for two minutes and then add garlic and basil
Set aside the cooked eggplant

Preheat the mini waffle maker if needed
Mix cooked eggplant, eggs, and 1 cup mozzarella cheese properly
Spread it to the mini waffle maker thoroughly
Cook for 4 minutes or till it turns crispy and then remove it from the waffle maker
Make as many mini chaffles as you can
Now in a baking tray, line these mini chaffles and top with the tomato sauce and grated mozzarella cheese
Put the tray in the oven at 400 degrees until the cheese melts
Serve hot

## 145. Jalapeno Eggplant Chaffle

Servings: 2
Preparation Time: 10 minutes
Total Time: 15 minutes

**What You Need:**

Eggplant: ½ cup diced and boiled
Onion powder: 1/4 tsp
Garlic powder: 1/4 tsp
Egg: 1
Cheddar cheese: 1/4 cup
Jalapeno: 1 diced
Cream cheese: 1 tbsp
Parmesan cheese: 1/8 tbsps
Salt: as per your taste

**How To Cook:**

Preheat a mini waffle maker if needed and grease it

In a mixing bowl, beat egg and add all the ingredients
Mix them all well
Pour the mixture to the lower plate of the waffle maker and spread it evenly to cover the plate properly
Close the lid
Cook for at least 4 minutes to get the desired crunch
Remove the chaffle from the heat and keep aside for around one minute
Make as many chaffles as your mixture and waffle maker allow
Serve hot and enjoy

# TURKEY CHAFFLES

## 146. Turkey Burger Chaffle

Servings: 2
Preparation Time: 15 minutes
Total Time: 20 minutes
**What You Need:**
**For the Chaffle:**
Egg: 2
Mozzarella Cheese: 1 cup (shredded)
Butter: 1 tbsp
Almond flour: 2 tbsp
Turmeric: ¼ tsp
Baking powder: ¼ tsp
Xanthan gum: a pinch
Onion powder: a pinch
Garlic powder: a pinch
Salt: a pinch
**For the Turkey:**
Ground turkey: 1 lb
Chives: 2 tbsp
Halloumi cheese: 1 cup
Salt: ¼ tsp or as per your taste
Black pepper: ¼ tsp or as per your taste

**How To Cook:**
Mix all the turkey ingredient in a bowl
Make patties either grill them or fry them
Preheat a mini waffle maker if needed and grease it
In a mixing bowl, add all the chaffle ingredients and mix well
Pour the mixture to the lower plate of the waffle maker and spread it evenly to cover the plate properly and close the lid
Cook for at least 4 minutes to get the desired crunch
Remove the chaffle from the heat and keep aside for around one minute
Make as many chaffles as your mixture and waffle maker allow
Serve with the turkey patties in between of two chaffles

## 147. Turkey Garlic Chaffle Roll

Servings: 2
Preparation Time: 20 minutes
Total Time: 40 minutes

**What You Need:**
Turkey mince: 1 cup
Salt: ¼ tsp or as per your taste
Black pepper: ¼ tsp or as per your taste
Egg: 2
Lemon juice: 1 tbsp
Water: 1/2 cup
Mozzarella Cheese: 1 cup (shredded)

Butter: 2 tbsp
Garlic powder: 1½ tsp
Bay seasoning: ½ tsp
Parsley: for garnishing

**How To Cook:**
In a frying pan, melt butter and add the turkey mince
Add ½ cup water for the mince to tender
When done, add salt, pepper, 1 tbsp garlic powder, and lemon juice and set aside

In a mixing bowl, beat eggs and add mozzarella cheese to them with ½ garlic powder and bay seasoning

Mix them all well and pour to the greasy mini waffle maker

Cook for at least 4 minutes to get the desired crunch

Remove the chaffle from the heat, add the turkey mixture in between and fold

Make as many chaffles as your mixture and waffle maker allowTop with parsley

Serve hot and enjoy!

## 148. Green Turkey Chaffle

Servings: 4
Preparation Time: 10 minutes
Total Time: 45 minutes

**What You Need:**
Turkey: 1/3 cup boiled and shredded
Cabbage: 1/3 cup
Broccoli: 1/3 cup
Zucchini: 1/3 cup
Egg: 2
Mozzarella Cheese: 1 cup (shredded)
Butter: 1 tbsp
Onion powder: a pinch
Garlic powder: a pinch
Salt: a pinch

**How To Cook:**
In a deep saucepan, boil cabbage, broccoli, and zucchini for five minutes or till it tenders, strain and blend

Mix all the remaining ingredients well together

Pour a thin layer on a preheated waffle iron

Add a layer of the blended vegetables on the mixture

Again add more mixture over the top

Cook the chaffle for around 5 minutes

Serve with your favorite sauce

## 149. Turkey Jalapeno Chaffle

Servings: 2
Preparation Time: 10 minutes
Total Time: 30 minutes

**What You Need:**
Turkey mince: ½ cup
Onion powder: 1/8 tsp
Garlic powder: 1/8 tsp
Egg: 1

Salt: as per your taste
Cheddar cheese: 1/4 cup
Jalapeno: 1 diced
Cream cheese: 1 tbsp
Butter: 1 tbsp
Parmesan cheese: 1/8 tbsp

**How To Cook:**

Cook the turkey meat on low flame with butter

Preheat a mini waffle maker if needed and grease it

In a mixing bowl, beat eggs and add all the ingredients including prepared turkey

Mix them all well

Pour the mixture to the lower plate of the waffle maker and spread it evenly to cover the plate properly

Close the lid

Cook for at least 4 minutes to get the desired crunch

Remove the chaffle from the heat and keep aside for around one minute

Make as many chaffles as your mixture and waffle maker allow

Serve hot and enjoy!

## 150. Turkey BBQ Chaffle

Servings: 2
Preparation Time: 10 minutes
Total Time: 30 minutes

**What You Need:**
Turkey meat: 1/2 cup
Butter: 1 tbsp
BBQ sauce: 1 tbsp (sugar-free)
Almond flour: 2 tbsp
Egg: 1
Cheddar cheese: ½ cup

**How To Cook:**
Cook the turkey meat in the butter on a low-medium heat for 10 minutes

Preheat your waffle iron

In mixing bowl, add all the chaffle ingredients including turkey meat and mix well

Grease your waffle iron lightly

Pour the mixture to the bottom plate evenly; also spread it out to get better results and close the upper plate and heat

Cook for 6 minutes or until the chaffle is done

Make as many chaffles as your mixture and waffle maker allow

Servings: 2
Preparation Time: 15 minutes
Total Time: 25 minutes

**What You Need:**

Turkey: 1 cup
Egg: 2
Mozzarella cheese: 1 cup and 4 tbsp
Tomato sauce: 6 tbsp
Basil: ½ tsp
Garlic: ½ tbsp
Butter: 1 tsp

**How To Cook:**

In a pan, add butter and include small pieces of turkey to it
Stir for two minutes and then add garlic and basil
Set aside the cooked turkey

Preheat the mini waffle maker if needed
Mix cooked turkey, eggs, and 1 cup mozzarella cheese properly
Spread it to the mini waffle maker thoroughly
Cook for 4 minutes or till it turns crispy and then remove it from the waffle maker
Make as many mini chaffles as you can
Now in a baking tray, line these mini chaffles and top with the tomato sauce and grated mozzarella cheese
Put the tray in the oven at 400 degrees until the cheese melts
Serve hot

## Conclusion

If you follow the ketogenic diet, with the dishes offered by this book, you can still enjoy delicious food, while keeping low your carb intake. The recipes found here are really low-carb, and the goal is to use the pure and natural ingredients to give a taste of your dishes.

Thank you and good luck!

*Amanda Hayden*

Made in the USA
Columbia, SC
03 September 2020